# The Secrets to Writing Great Comedy

Teach® Yourself

# The Secrets to Writing Great Comedy

Lesley Bown

Hodder Education

338 Euston Road, London NW1 3BH.

Hodder Education is an Hachette UK company

First published in UK 2011 by Hodder Education

First published in US 2011 by The McGraw-Hill Companies, Inc.

Copyright © Lesley Bown 2011

Database right Hodder Education (makers)

The Teach Yourself name is a registered trademark of Hachette UK.

British Library Cataloguing in Publication Data: a catalogue record
for this title is available from the British Library.

Library of Congress Catalog Card Number: on file.

10 9 8 7 6 5 4 3 2

The publisher has used its best endeavours to ensure that any
website addresses referred to in this book are correct and active at
the time of going to press. However, the publisher and the author
have no responsibility for the websites and can make no guarantee
that a site will remain live or that the content will remain relevant,
decent or appropriate.

The publisher has made every effort to mark as such all words
which it believes to be trademarks. The publisher should also
like to make it clear that the presence of a word in the book,
whether marked or unmarked, in no way affects its legal status as
a trademark.

Every reasonable effort has been made by the publisher to trace the
copyright holders of material in this book. Any errors or omissions
should be notified in writing to the publisher, who will endeavour
to rectify the situation for any reprints and future editions.

Hachette UK's policy is to use papers that are natural, renewable
and recyclable products, and made from wood grown in sustainable
forests. The logging and manufacturing processes are expected to
conform to the environmental regulations of the country of origin.

www.hoddereducation.co.uk

Typeset by MPS Limited, a Macmillan Company.

Printed and bound by CPI Group (UK) Ltd, Croydon, CR0 4YY

*For Nicky, Rob and Kerry, because you make me laugh.*

# Acknowledgments

Thanks to everyone who helped with this book, and special thanks to Alan Ayckbourn, Simon Brett, Eric Chappell, Ray Cooney, Jan Etherington, Ann Gawthorpe, Mindy Glazer, Rob Grant, Candy Guard, Miranda Hart, Paul Hayes-Watkins, Sue Limb, Chris Ritchie, Ken Rock, Victoria Roddam, Tony Staveacre, Count Arthur Strong, Kev F Sutherland and Mike Vardy.

# Contents

# Meet the author

It started, as these things often do, innocently enough. There was a noticeboard in the main school corridor where we pinned up announcements of netball matches, choir practices and play rehearsals. I added a short humorous piece, which turned out to be the equivalent of lighting the blue touch paper. Luckily I was standing well back when the hordes descended. Eventually crowd control was instigated, each group being allowed five minutes before they were moved on.

It was a pre-Internet example of viral marketing. The first reader was one of the new kids, barely tall enough to see the board, who beetled off and told her friends, so that then there were five, then ten, and by the end of lunch break mass hysteria was breaking out.

It was a heady experience, and it also taught me something about the strange place comedy writers occupy in the world. The teachers, even before they'd wiped the grins from their faces, were at great pains to tell me that it was All Very Well Young Lady, but Real Life is a Serious Business.

Nothing has changed. I am still pinning comedy up on the metaphorical noticeboard, and I am still not serious enough for Real Life. Unreal Life, on the other hand, is a great place to be.

Lesley Bown

# *In one minute*

The single most important factor in making people laugh is to take them by surprise. Laughter is a response to the shock of the unexpected, so anything incongruous is likely to be funny.

We all have expectations about other people, so undermining those expectations creates instant incongruity. For instance, we expect a certain kind of behaviour and language from a doctor. For comedy purposes, a doctor who talks and behaves like a used car salesman or a streetwise teenager is bound to be funny. The bigger the gap between the two, the greater the comedy potential.

To practise creating this type of incongruity, try this simple exercise. First choose a character from list A and another from list B:

▶ List A: doctor, maths teacher, High Court judge, politician
▶ List B: used car salesman, streetwise teenager, hairdresser, plumber.

Now write a short speech for one of the characters using the type of language you'd expect from the other character. For instance, the doctor could be looking at a patient's operation scar and saying 'What cowboy did this then? I could sort it out but it won't be easy, can't get the parts you see, could fit you in Tuesday week, cash in hand alright with you Squire?' and so on. Choose your own incongruous characters and try the exercise again. You can use specific people (e.g. the Prime Minister) or fictional characters (e.g. Robin Hood).

# Introduction

This is not a funny book. There are plenty of funny books out there, but this isn't one of them, because comedy writing is a serious business. Mind you, the first rule of comedy writing is 'never tell your audience that you're going to make them laugh' so perhaps this is a funny book after all, and I just don't want to tell you in case you don't laugh. The only way to find out is to read the book.

There are multiple theories as to why we laugh. Is laughter a relief from repression, a safety valve for aggression, a way of bonding or a yell of victory? And is comedy a coping mechanism when times are tough, a way of cutting authority figures down to size or a way of enjoying the misfortunes of others? Is it about reinforcing shared values or about feeling superior? Why do we laugh equally at witty wordplay and yucky sick jokes? And why do we laugh when we're tickled?

Luckily you can write comedy without knowing the answers to these questions, although it does help to understand the basics of humour.

Most art simply doesn't survive. Jane Austen is still popular but who now reads Fanny Burney, Nancy Russell Mitford or Maria Edgeworth, all contemporaries of hers? Austen survives partly because she was an outstandingly good writer, but also because she chose subjects that still resonate with us today. In other words there must be an element of luck. Just like Jane Austen you can only write about what interests you, and there is no way of knowing who will share that interest or for how long.

Comedy is even more ephemeral than other types of art, because it is so much about what is happening now, and because it only really works if it can be grasped more or less instantly. Even the laugh that comes from a joke that needs a little thought is only a few seconds behind the punchline.

When Dorothy Parker was told 'Calvin Coolidge is dead' she reportedly replied 'How can they tell?' This is only funny if you happen to know that Calvin Coolidge was an American President famous for his lack of small talk and deadpan manner. Of course the joke can be endlessly recycled but very few people now will relish the original.

You can see from the Calvin Coolidge joke that comedy often does more than just make us laugh – it tells us something about our culture. Since culture changes over time, and so do the ways in which we see ourselves as a nation, comedy will also change. This matters more to some writers than others. P. G. Wodehouse somehow managed to transcend the area of British culture he wrote about, and his books are still funny today decades after its disappearance. It remains to be seen whether the same will be true of Alan Bennett and Victoria Wood, although I sincerely hope that it will be. It is certainly true that much comedy depends on shared values and shared cultural reference points.

There are also shared taboos. These are culture specific, although some must be more universal than others. They also change over time, so what seems politically correct to us now will be all wrong in 50 years' time. Taboos are not, incidentally, anything to do with whether something is funny or not. A joke can be screamingly funny but if it's not acceptable to the audience then it won't raise a titter.

The better news is that scientists have definitely proved that laughing is good for us, and we all need to do more of it. It's quite hard to laugh at nothing so we need comedy writers and performers to create laughter for us. One of the odd things about laughter is that we don't laugh so easily at real events. If we see someone slip on a banana skin, we rush to help them up, but we're willing to laugh at an actor doing the same thing. The world of comedy is an artificial environment in which laughter is permitted because nothing is real.

Like I said, it's a serious business. Start by doing some research. Consume as much comedy as you can. If it makes you laugh, work out why. If it doesn't make you laugh, work out why. If anyone suggests you're spending too much time enjoying comedy, explain that it's research.

That's the upside of comedy writing. For the downside, read this book. No, that's not quite what I meant. This isn't a funny book, but it won't be a depressing read either. You'll find clear explanations of the various elements of comedy, and exercises to help you practise what you've learnt. You won't find much about my personal taste in comedy. Like most people I have strong preferences but that's not the point. There are many different audiences for many different types of comedy, and all are equally worthwhile.

You also won't find any swearing, sexual or religious jokes in the examples. My personal taboos may be tighter or looser than yours, but as far as possible I've tried to write a book that is accessible to everyone. Once you've learnt how to do it, you can apply it to whatever kind of comedy floats your boat.

The examples are mostly taken from comedy classics, simply because most readers will already be familiar with them, and in any case they're easily accessible. The invented examples are aimed to make the point rather than hit the comedy heights.

When I say 'audience' I mean anyone who is on the receiving end of comedy. Whether they're in a theatre or cinema, reading a book or magazine, listening to the radio or an audiobook, or at home watching TV, they are an 'audience' as far as this book is concerned. I've occasionally used 'listener' or 'reader' where I need to be very specific, but otherwise 'audience' it is.

Finally, scattered throughout the book are two sorts of Insight. Author Insights, based on my experiences, and Comedy Insights, which were very kindly given to me by other comedy professionals. I've kept these exactly as they were sent, word for word, and you'll see from reading them that there is more than one approach to comedy writing.

Let's get started, and let's start with an exercise.

## Exercise

Write down everything that's made you laugh today. Describe in detail, and say why you laughed. If nothing made you laugh, look back to yesterday, or the day before. If you have to go back more than a week, perhaps comedy writing isn't for you.

# Part one
# Writing

*People must be amuthed, Thquire, thomehow... they can't be alwayth working, nor yet they can't be alwayth learning.*

Charles Dickens, *Hard Times*

# 1

# Comedy basics

In this chapter you will learn:
- *about surprise and recognition*
- *about creating laughs*
- *about visual, verbal and physical comedy.*

---

**Comedy insight – ALAN AYCKBOURN**

*If I had to give just one piece of comedy writing advice it would be: for God's sake take it seriously.*

Alan Ayckbourn is a Director and Playwright

---

It's pretty difficult to fake laughter, ask any actor. It's also hard to stop once you've started – again, actors will tell you about the nightmare of corpsing, when they get the giggles and can't stop. It can be just as hard to get started if you're not in the mood. We really don't have much control over laughing – perhaps that's why we value it so much.

So what makes us laugh? Or rather, what is there in common between the various things that make us laugh?

The two main factors are surprise and recognition. Most laughs come from surprise: the sudden unexpected event, the twist that you didn't see coming, the moment when the penny drops. We usually laugh at moments of recognition in a less explosive, more thoughtful way. It's a rueful 'yes, I do that too' sort of laugh.

Observational comedy makes great use of recognition precisely because it is based on everyday life, but to be successful it has to include some surprises too. Recognition laughs are very useful as laughs along the way, as you build up to the big surprise punchline.

A lot of surprise laughs are created when an audience thinks they recognize what's about to happen, and are taken by surprise by what actually does happen. The key concept in creating both surprise and recognition laughs is incongruity, because the incongruous is also the unexpected. This works at every level of comedy, from the simplest joke to the most complex plot.

**Exercise**

To practise creating surprise, have a go at this Job Applications Exercise.

Who would be the worst possible applicants for these jobs: heart transplant surgeon, TV weather forecaster, massage therapist? There are no correct answers, but whatever you choose will only be funny if it's surprising.

---

# Creating laughs

Let's look at ways of creating incongruity, surprise and recognition in more detail.

### OPPOSITES

Opposites provide instant incongruity: big and small, happy and sad, funerals and weddings. This is why double acts often exaggerate the physical differences between them; for instance, Laurel was thin and Hardy was fat. Casting of *Only Fools and Horses* must have been helped by the eight inch height difference between David Jason and Nicholas Lyndhurst. Of course sometimes this can be an illusion – neither Morecambe nor Wise was a particularly big man but much was made of Wise being the shorter of the two.

### MISDIRECTION

Misdirection is when a joke or situation creates an expectation in the audience, and instead of meeting the expectation you deliver something different and surprising. It's very common in wordplay jokes:

> *I'm sure wherever my granny is, she's looking down on us. She's not dead, just very condescending.*

### INVERSION

Turning things around, or looking at them backwards, creates incongruity – for instance, a tough guy who's scared of spiders or a child with more sense than its parents.

### MISUNDERSTANDING

Misunderstanding is a staple of comedy plotting. It's often thought of as primarily a vehicle for farce but is actually used all the time in sitcoms, including the classics such as *Frasier* and *Fawlty Towers*. For instance, there's an episode of *Coupling* where Jane is asked round to dinner and decides to snare her man by wearing nothing under her coat – and then discovers it's actually a dinner party.

You can get a laugh if the audience learns the truth at the same time as the character, but you can also choose to let the audience in on the secret. A good example of this is in Alan Ayckbourn's play *Absurd Person Singular*. In the second act Eve is trying to commit suicide – the audience quickly realize this but none of the characters do, although each time she tries, they manage, without realizing, to prevent her.

### EXAGGERATION

Exaggeration is an obvious comic tool but needs to be used very precisely as it has an effect on the tone of the piece. Look at the differences between Jim Carrey's exaggerated performance in *Ace Ventura Pet Detective* and his far more subtle approach in *The Truman Show*. It's exactly the same with writing – the more you exaggerate, the broader the comedy.

### DOUBLE ENTENDRE

Our appetite for double entendre, or innuendo, seems bottomless, despite the fact we simultaneously acknowledge that it is extremely childish and not really funny at all. Of course it's possible to create double entendres that aren't smutty but there isn't too much comedy value in them. The more censorship and repression there is, the more double entendre flourishes.

### BATHOS

Bathos is the move from the sublime to the ridiculous. It's another form of exaggeration because it works by exaggerating the contrast between the two. For instance the movie *Shaun of the Dead* takes the horror movie genre and sets it in boring suburban London rather than a spooky castle, a deserted wood at midnight or any other conventional horror setting.

### THE RULE OF THREE

There is something about the rhythm of threes in speech that really works – faith, hope and charity, or *Sex, Lies and Videotape*. In comedy this seems to be a simple case of set-up, establishment and punchline. So you start your list with the set-up, the second item establishes that this is a list and prepares the audience for the third item, the funny one:

> *It was a very old plane. It was held together by Faith, Hope and Chewing Gum.*

Or you can make all the items funny but build to the third one:

> *It was a very old plane. It was held together by sticky tape, string and dinosaur sweat.*

The audience will anticipate that the third element will be funny, but even so, you have to find a way to surprise them with it.

### AND FINALLY...

There is a whole raft of words and objects that are perceived to be incongruous and therefore funny without any rational explanation – in other words, it's a mystery why they are funny. The list changes over time and has cultural variations. Using these words and objects adds texture to your writing although they aren't generally used in punchlines.

K is the funniest letter of the alphabet and 32 is the funniest number. Hamsters are funnier than cats, chip shops are funnier than carpet shops and so on. Sometimes analysts attempt explanation – K is a plosive consonant, 32 sounds funny in certain accents, cats are culturally perceived as elegant and intelligent whereas hamsters aren't, and so on. Mostly these feel unconvincing, and as a writer you only need to know what gets laughs.

Exercise

Make your own list of words and objects you find funny.

## Visual, verbal and physical

The three broad categories of comedy are visual, verbal and physical.

Visual comedy is anything that creates a picture for the audience, whether it's performers carrying out actions laid down in a script, or a word picture in a novel. Verbal comedy relies on wordplay. Physical comedy is entirely about performance.

### VISUAL COMEDY

Word pictures can create jokes that would be beyond the physical capabilities of most performers or are even physically impossible. In other words they range from the almost realistic:

> *I slept like a log last night, I woke up in the fireplace.*

to the totally surreal:

> *Last night I dreamed I was eating a huge marshmallow. When I woke up the pillow was gone.*

If you're writing for performance you'll need to describe the actions and props that will produce the visual laughs, and if you're writing prose you'll need to create funny pictures to amuse your readers. Also make sure the actions are physically possible. Test them out yourself just in case you've written something that needs three hands to be accomplished.

You'll find more about creating word pictures as you read on.

### VERBAL COMEDY

Verbal jokes usually depend on some sort of wordplay such as a pun. Although they're often clever they're not usually screamingly funny, so they work best if they are slotted in to a word picture that is funny.

Simple wordplay is often used to create a light atmosphere, such as a hairdresser's called *Hair Today* or a chip shop called *The Fish Plaice*. These can also make jokes:

> *A subservient fish knows his plaice.*

but they're more likely to get a groan than a laugh. To get a laugh you need a visual element:

> *There's a new portable stereo on the market that looks like a chocolate cake. It's called a gateaux blaster.*

You'll also find more about verbal comedy as you read on.

### PHYSICAL COMEDY

Physical comedy is ancient, accessible and transcends language. It's easy to assume that there isn't much call for writers of physical comedy – isn't it up to the performer to just go out there and be funny? However when I tell you that there are three writers listed for *Mr Bean*, you'll see that someone has to think up all that funny business. Writers can expect to work in close collaboration with the performers as they will have individual abilities and limitations.

Physical comedy comes from two sources: the comedian him- or herself and the comedian's interaction with the world.

Obviously it helps if the performer looks funny in some way, but more often than not this is an illusion created by posture, facial expression and clothes. Look at Rowan Atkinson as Mr Bean and as Blackadder and you'll see how this works.

Interactions with the world can be with other people, animals and objects.

One of the key types of interaction involves violence. For some reason we love to laugh at the most extreme sufferings of other people, and physical comedians can expect to be assaulted in endless ways.

Another important type of interaction involves helpless clumsiness. The rest of the world, whether animate or inanimate, is a puzzle that can never be solved – taps won't turn on then suddenly gush water, gates won't open, chairs collapse and technology never works.

Mime is a highly specialized form of visual performance which can be funny but also moving, serious and profound. Performers traditionally use white face paint and tight black clothing and are often street performers. However a more modern take on mime is possible. Rowan Atkinson playing an invisible drum kit or piano is not strictly mime as there is a sound accompaniment, but it is very very funny.

*Exercise*

Take an everyday object and see how many funny things can be done with it, both clumsy and violent.

---

**Comedy insight – COUNT ARTHUR STRONG**
*The most common mistake that new comedy writers make is trying not to make mistakes. Making mistakes is good. Don't worry about it. It's a fine way of learning.*

Count Arthur Strong, via Steve Delaney

---

## Things to remember

▶ Laughter is triggered by surprise and recognition.

▶ We laugh at the incongruous.

▶ Observational comedy relies on recognition but needs surprise as well.

▶ Comedy uses opposites, misdirection, inversion, misunderstanding, exaggeration, double entendre, bathos and threes.

▶ Don't forget the mystery element.

▶ Comedy can be visual, verbal or physical.

# 2

Comedy writing mindset

In this chapter you will learn:
- *about the three factors in comedy*
- *how to organize your writing life*
- *about dos and don'ts.*

There is a big difference between enjoying comedy and writing comedy. Sounds obvious, but just think about it for a moment. Plenty of people who love food are hopeless cooks themselves. Most spectators at the Cup Final are not great footballers. And how many rock music lovers never get further than playing air guitar?

> **Comedy insight – ROB GRANT**
>
> *The most common mistake that new comedy writers make is thinking that things that are funny in real life are going to be equally funny in a script, without any adjustments. Just because something actually happened doesn't mean it's believable. When football commentators say 'You couldn't write this', what they really mean is 'If you wrote this, everyone would think it was contrived and incredible and really, really bad writing.'*
>
> Rob Grant is a love lord, writer, producer and *Red Dwarf* co-creator

Of course, if you don't actually enjoy comedy then perhaps you need to think again. Any kind of writing is hard work, and the rewards are uncertain. If you're buying into a dream of fame and fortune, then look for an easier route.

On the other hand, if you struggled in English lessons at school, don't let that stop you. You don't have to worry if your spelling is hopeless, as you can use a spellchecker to iron out most of the mistakes.

Writing comedy is not about passing exams or being top of the class. It's about making people laugh, and for that you'll need a comedy writing mindset.

Comedy is created by three factors: the audience, the medium and the material. You can think of this as a triangle, because the three are inextricably linked, and the top point of the triangle belongs to the audience. Without them, there is no comedy.

Exercise

Collect 20 jokes. Work out why they're funny.

## The audience

Initially you'll write for yourself. Everybody does. When you begin to write for an audience you'll have started the journey from amateur to professional. If you are the only person who finds your work funny then you won't have much of a future as a comedy writer. You're entitled to your opinion of course, we all are.

### DEFINING YOUR AUDIENCE

'The audience' is whoever is on the receiving end of your work. It might be hundreds of people watching a live performance, or one person alone in their bedsit reading your novel. Whoever they are, you'll need to reach them and have respect for them. That doesn't mean buttering them up, but it does mean making them laugh.

Initially your audience will almost certainly be people like you. If you're an angst-ridden teenage boy or a harassed mother you'll find it easiest to reach out to people in the same situation as you. You know how it feels, you know what they're going through and you'll instinctively understand the humour of the situation. When Spike Milligan wrote *The Goon Show* he drew on his experience in the Army during the Second World War. All comedy is specific in this way.

At the same time you'll find there is a universal element. If you write about being young, then older people will use their own memories to connect with your comedy. If you write about being old, then young people will think about older people they know. When *The Goon Show* was first broadcast the entire nation knew something of military life and could connect with it.

What this all means is that basically you'll have a core audience, of people like you, and a wider audience of people who can connect with your humour in some way, at some level.

### REACHING YOUR AUDIENCE

The question is, how do you reach your audience? There are some direct routes – open mic nights (if you're willing to perform), blogs, self-published novels – but on the whole you'll find that you have to go via someone else. This could be a book publisher, a magazine editor, a radio producer, a commissioning editor at a TV production company or a theatre script reader. All of these people stand between you and your audience, and it can be quite annoying to find that you have to persuade them to take you on before you can even think about reaching your actual target.

All I can say is, just accept it, that's how it is. These people have power, but they also have responsibility. Some of them have mega-bucks to spend and all of them have their jobs on the line if they mess up. Almost all of them are looking for the Next Big Thing, although some may be after a quirkier take that will only ever find a niche audience.

So start by writing what you want to write, what amuses you and what you'd like to see, read or hear. Then learn how to modify and improve it to reach a bigger audience. That is the heart of the difference between amateur and professional. Amateurs sit back when they've finished writing, amazed and delighted with themselves, and fully expecting the world to beat a pathway to their door. Professionals are equally amazed and delighted, but have learnt not to have those expectations. After a short break, they set about polishing and rewriting until the work is ready for public exposure.

## The medium

Do you want to write for performance or publication? For TV or theatre? Book publishing or journalism? No doubt you already know which medium you're drawn to, and while there is some crossover, there are also important differences. Jokes that work on the page are nothing on the screen, and vice versa.

The experience of being a writer differs between media as well. Journalists are on much shorter deadlines than novelists. All forms of performance are team efforts, and you'll need to be able to accept input from other people. The performer is the means by which the material is delivered to the audience so in that sense the performer is the medium, and you'll have to take that into account.

## The material

This is the point of the triangle that belongs to you, the comedy writer. It's what this book is about. Let's start with the basics.

Exercise

Watch a recorded episode of any sitcom. Write out what happens in each scene and what makes it funny.

**Author insight**

I was at a University drinks do, chatting and laughing with a group of people that included David Lodge, the novelist and playwright. Suddenly he said to one of us 'now that's funny – you don't mind if I use it do you?' A comedy writer is never off duty.

### NOTEBOOK

This simple low-tech device will soon become your best friend. Have one that's small enough to slip into a pocket, along with a pencil (almost anything else is likely to leak into your pocket). If you're a techno-geek you might like an electronic gizmo, but on the whole pencil and paper is easier and cheaper. And then use your notebook to – yes, that's right – make notes. Don't rely on your memory. When you see or hear something amusing, or an idea pops into your head out of the blue, get it written down pronto.

There is one drawback to the notebook concept, which is that I find ideas tend to flow when I'm driving and obviously can't write anything down. Even groping for a little recording device is not recommended. I've never found a solution to that one.

Also of course (alright, two drawbacks), notebooks are easy to lose. That's why you need to move the notes onto your laptop or PC regularly. All of which brings us to:

### TIME

Making time for transcribing your notes is only the start of it. You will need time to write, time to rewrite, time to network, time to send material out and so on. If you really want to get your comedy out there, you'll need to be organized as well as creative and you'll need to find time for both aspects of the work. But rather than worry about this, approach it from the other direction. Decide how much time you have available and work with that.

It's a good idea to formally set time aside for writing. Waiting till you have a free moment, or having vague ideas about when you'll write, is very unlikely to be productive. Look at your life and decide where you can make time for writing. However busy you are, you should be able to juggle your timetable. Maybe you can cut down the time you spend watching TV, get up earlier, or stay up later. If you're a commuter, can you write on the train? If you're a parent, how about the time you spend waiting while your kids are at an activity?

### FRIENDS IN HIGH PLACES

It's easy enough, after a few rejections, to feel you're bashing your head against a locked and bolted door that will never open. Looking at other, more successful writers, you start to wonder if they were somebody's relative, or went to school with somebody, or had some other way in that isn't fair. There's no point in getting bogged down with this one. Having friends in high places will quite possibly unlock that door and open it a crack, but that's all. Once through the door you still have deliver the comedy and the audience still have to like it.

In any case, you can find your own way through. It's called networking. Get out there and meet people – start with your local comedy scene. Build up relationships, establish a reputation for being funny, hardworking and reliable, and sooner or later the door will start to swing open.

Look through a newspaper or magazine and study the cartoons. Decide what makes them funny.

### WORKING WITH OTHER PEOPLE

There's a long tradition of comedy writers working in pairs: Muir and Nordon, Galton and Simpson, Dick Clement and Ian La Frenais, French and Saunders. Even the five Pythons worked as two writing pairs and a singleton. It seems to work for comedy because you can test the material on each other and know straightaway if it gets a laugh. It works really well if you each have different talents, and it's not so good if you have the same strengths and weaknesses.

To work in a pair you have to have a level of trust in each other, so that each one feels free to say anything, however lame and unfunny it turns out to be. If you're worried about getting a sarky put-down from the other person then you'll seize up and find it hard to let the ideas flow. It also doesn't help if you get competitive with each other and you'll need a way of dealing with arguments.

**Author insight**

I've worked with three different writers and we made copious use of email, but it soon became apparent that only one person should work on the piece at a time, otherwise you end up with multiple versions.

## Comedy mindset dos and don'ts

'Dos and don'ts' may sound like a whole bunch of rules, but as with everything in this book think of them more as a series of guidelines. If you can ignore them and still be successful, that's fine, but for most writers, especially when they first start out, working within the guidelines is the best way forward.

**Don't try to be funny,** at least, not when you first start work. Write down everything you think of, whether it's funny, tragic or just plain boring. If you limit yourself to only looking for funny ideas you'll dam up the creative juices.

**Do keep everything you write.** When things aren't going well, frustration can make you screw up the paper and throw it in the bin, or delete the file. Don't do that, as you just never know what might be useful later on. Build up a joke collection for future reference.

**Do stay up to date with popular culture.** As soon as a new gadget appears on the market, a new TV programme becomes popular or a new catchphrase is doing the rounds, you will find opportunities for new jokes.

**Do have an opinion on everything.** There isn't much comedy in the balanced viewpoint.

**Do be a comedy consumer.** Watch sitcoms, go to open mic nights, see comedy at the theatre, read funny books, look at the cartoons in newspapers and magazines. Don't confine yourself to your favourites, have a look at everything.

**Do keep going till it's really funny.** A lot of comedy writers say they don't get anything really funny till around the seventh attempt. The outstanding writers don't stop there, they keep going. The harder you push yourself, the funnier it gets.

**Do read your work out loud.** Whether it's a novel or a sitcom, you need to listen to the rhythms of your writing.

**Do be prepared to work hard.** No one ever said it was going to be an easy ride.

**Comedy insight – JAN ETHERINGTON**

*Read it aloud! That way, you discover if your dialogue is real or if you are writing 'sitcom' speak. You'll hear the rhythm of your characters' voices and learn to recognize – and banish – 'Harry The Explainer' i.e. clunky exposition – 'Brian is your brother. He may be younger than you and still a student but he can't help it if Sylvia finds him attractive, even though she was once engaged to you.'*

Jan Etherington is an award-winning comedy writer, broadcaster and journalist

Exercise

Play the superheroes game. Invent superheroes with bizarre supernatural gifts and work out how they would save the planet.

## Things to remember

▶ Comedy is created by the audience, the medium and the material.

▶ Comedy is specific but has a universal element.

▶ Don't rely on your memory, keep a notebook to hand.

▶ Make time for writing and stick to it.

▶ Networking creates opportunities.

▶ Comedy writers often work in pairs.

▶ Don't strain to be funny but do keep going till you get there.

▶ Keep up to date with comedy, culture and current affairs.

▶ Read your work out loud.

# 3

# Getting started

In this chapter you will learn:
- *about anarchy and discipline*
- *where to look for ideas.*

Whatever type of comedy you plan to write you will need to generate funny ideas, write them out, and polish them. In the course of doing this you'll create a lot of material that won't be relevant to your current project. Keep it. Keep everything. If you start to be successful as a writer, you'll have a ready-made fund of material to draw on.

You'll soon devise your own way of working. Some writers like to plan everything in detail, others like to plunge in and see where the writing takes them. You certainly don't have to start at the beginning and work through to the end; in fact it's best to draft out anything that is nagging at you so that you clear your head. Don't however spend time polishing it until you've got a complete draft because you're bound to have to cut some stuff.

## Comedy insight – CANDY GUARD

*If I had to give just one piece of comedy writing advice, it would be to train your brain to observe your own responses to everything and anything, however painful or ridiculous. Then be brutally honest. That means learning to laugh at yourself, the hardest lesson of all. Take the funniest bits, test them on a few friends and package them up neatly. Then be generous and admit them to your audience, encouraging them to have the same liberating experience, yet with a comforting sense of 'Thank God! It's not just me!'*

Candy Guard is a comic artist (*Pond Life*, the *Observer*)

The basic stages of writing are:

1 Generate ideas.
2 Write a draft.
3 Rewrite and polish.

All three require you to be both creative and hardworking. You'll need that exhilarating mix of anarchy and discipline that all artists use in their work.

## Anarchy

All comedy is anarchic in that it undermines the status quo and allows people to get away with outrageous behaviour that breaks all the social rules. This is why comedy can be used with serious intent and to make political points, although often of course the anarchy is only there to create laughter. So whether it is Wee Jimmy Krankie getting laughs off mischief that would never be tolerated in a real child, or Malcolm Tucker showing the dark side of politics in *The Thick Of It*, there is always an element of anarchy.

Part of your task as a comedy writer is to unleash your inner anarchist. Let down all the barriers, and forget about taste, political correctness and the conventions of society. Think the unthinkable, say the unsayable. Doing this is enormously liberating, but remember, it is a writing exercise. I'm not suggesting you should try walking naked down your local High Street, although you'd certainly acquire plenty of comedy material if you did.

Another way of looking at the anarchic side of comedy is to think of it as playtime. Revert to childhood, forget your worries and just have fun. Let go of your social conditioning and be as rude, silly and disrespectful as you like.

**Author insight**

I find that spending time in this way, letting myself be anarchic and childlike, is like free therapy, one of the many benefits of being a comedy writer.

Use some writing sessions to generate ideas, allowing your mind to be as wild and free as possible. The only rule in these sessions is to record everything by writing it down or by using a voice recorder.

Before you start, take a moment to clear your mind of your everyday concerns, family worries, unpaid bills and so on. Even let go of your desires for this particular piece of writing. Forget about deadlines, who you're writing for (or would like to write for) and your acceptance speech when you win an award. All of these concerns will cramp you into a mental box and stop you going to the limits of possibility.

## Exercise

One way to get in touch with your inner anarchist is by playing silly games with other people. For instance, try the Forehead Game. Everyone writes the name of someone famous on a sticky note and the notes are stuck to people's foreheads without them seeing the name. Each person has a turn at guessing the name on their own forehead. They can ask any question but will only get Yes or No answers from the others. If the answer is No, the game moves on to the next person. Keep going till everyone knows the name on their forehead.

EXERCISE

----

**Comedy insight – MIRANDA HART**

*If I had to give just one piece of comedy writing advice it would be: write what you think is funny, don't try and appeal to a certain demographic or what you think the broadcasters might like.*

Miranda Hart is a comedy actress and writer

----

### GENERATING MATERIAL

Well, you've shut yourself away with pencil and paper and promised yourself a good dose of anarchy and playtime to get the ideas flowing. Except nothing happens. You feel self-conscious and awkward and not at all funny. Here are a few suggestions to kick-start the process.

When you're trying any of these techniques, don't pay any attention to the quality of the ideas. That comes later. All you need to do at first is get the ideas flowing. Most of them will be rubbish. Many of them will be embarrassingly bad. Don't worry about it – just be prepared to discard them during the editing process.

### FREE-THINKING

The classic way to free-think is to use a big piece of paper. Write your central topic in the middle and draw a circle round it, with lines radiating out. At the end of the lines write ideas connected with the topic, draw circles round them and lines radiating out, then add more connected words and so on. Don't restrict yourself or strain to be original – you can be both conventional and wacky since both might lead to something useful. In fact don't censor anything. That comes later in a discipline session.

There doesn't seem to be a way to free-think on the computer but there are websites that offer online approaches.

### LISTS

No, not the dreaded To-Do list. Lists of almost anything can be used to generate ideas and are the comedy writer's great standby. Rather like free-thinking, you can make a list of words associated with a single topic, or you can take one word and see how many different topics it can be associated with.

Exercise

Make a shopping list of random objects and see if you can write a short paragraph that features all of them.

---

**Comedy insight – ROB GRANT**

*Study other comedy writers. Select writers whose work you admire, find anything you can they might have written or said in interviews about comedy writing, and deconstruct their work to try and figure out how they did it. Obviously, you shouldn't be copying them, but you'll be surprised what you can work out about technique and craft from them.*

Rob Grant is a love lord, writer, producer and *Red Dwarf* co-creator

---

# Discipline

Anarchy is only one side of the coin. All writing requires discipline once the initial wave of inspiration and enthusiasm has swept past. If you are writing for someone else, then you will need to meet their deadlines – the last thing you want is a reputation for being unreliable. Even if you're writing for yourself, you will need to keep on producing material, because the more you exercise your writing muscles, the stronger and more flexible they become.

This is also the time to put back some of the taste, social conventions and political correctness that you so gaily abandoned in the anarchy sessions. This is a matter of individual judgment and how you see yourself as a comedy writer. Do you want to shock, entertain or educate? It's up to you.

As you look through your material think of yourself as a miner in the Gold Rush, panning through the dirt and silt to find the tiny nuggets of gold. One difficulty is that you won't be able to use them all. You'll always have some wonderfully funny material that just isn't right for the piece you're working on. Just like gold, these nuggets will keep their value, so add them to your comedy file.

If you find yourself struggling to resolve problems in your writing, then revert to an anarchy session to help you think outside the box.

In comedy writing every word has to be there for a reason, and almost always the best way to get to the laugh is also the quickest. If you want to delay the laugh for some reason, then you have to give your audience something along the way – a smaller laugh, or something that keeps their interest.

Whether you're writing a one-liner or a novel you need to know how it's going to end. You may not know this when you first start writing, but at some point you'll realize where you're going. Once you know this, you need to revise everything you've written so far to make sure it relates to the ending in some way.

---

## Sources of comedy ideas

Comedy doesn't just appear from nowhere and most of the time it's no good waiting for inspiration to strike. If you want to write comedy, you have to go out and get some ideas. Luckily for you, they're all around.

### PEOPLE-WATCHING

Comedy is about people, and people are everywhere. Just keep your eyes and ears open and you'll soon start to gather material. Learn to sit quietly in public places and watch what is going on. Sometimes you can't help overhearing too.

### DAYDREAMING

Some would say this is the best bit of being writer. Lie back, close your eyes and let your thoughts drift. If you combine this with a hot bath then you can't be accused of time-wasting.

### EMOTIONS

A lot of comedy writing is driven by negative emotions. When you experience anger and frustration, look for the comedy in what has happened. For instance, there was a time when most stand-up routines seemed to include a rant about being put on hold, or about the menus on phone helplines. The frustrations of everyday life are great material, and so too are the bigger issues that arouse our anger.

Exercise

Make a list of things that make you angry, and explain why. These are your targets.

If you're going to use comedy as a vent for your emotions, then you need to be aware of certain boundaries. If the target of your comedy is in the audience, then only make jokes about things that aren't important to them personally. Think of a typical best man's speech at a wedding, which is full of digs at the bridegroom but would go badly wrong if it revealed unpleasant truths. Even if you feel justified in the attack, the effect will only be to make the audience uncomfortable and turn them against you and your message.

Of course in most comedy situations the targets aren't present, but there are still good and bad ways of being angry about them. Some targets are fair game, (politicians, the Royal family) and what they generally have in common is that they're perceived to be above the comedian and the audience in the social hierarchy. Generally when we find comedy objectionable, it's because it's aiming downwards rather than upwards. Undermining authority figures is acceptable, attacking the disadvantaged just isn't.

### FACE TIME

Getting together with other people can be a good way of generating ideas. You can socialize with your mates in a casual way or deliberately meet up with your comedy contacts to work on ideas. Expect a high wastage rate though. You'll find that a lot of jokes that seem hysterically funny at the pub after a couple of beers, turn out not to have any legs at all. Remember that private jokes among friends are always more extreme than public ones, and edit accordingly.

### FRIENDS AND FAMILY

Most of us find this one all too easy. Every family has a story to tell and most of these have comedy potential. How they will feel about you telling their story is quite another matter and outside the remit of this book.

### MEDIA

Here is another big advantage of being a writer. You really do need to watch a lot of TV, go to the theatre and cinema, and read newspapers and magazines. You're not idling, you're doing research. You can home in on current affairs, celebrities or any other aspect of our culture that interests you.

### OLD STORIES

Think of these as roughly everything that is out of copyright but still in general awareness, for example *Alice in Wonderland* or *Robinson Crusoe*. (Copyright lasts for an author's lifetime and for 70 years after their death). It also includes myths, folk tales and fairy stories.

With all of these you can retell the story with a modern twist, in the way that *West Side Story* was a retelling of *Romeo and Juliet* – of course you'll also be looking to make it funny. Another very useful comedy technique is to retell a story from the point of view of a minor character. For instance Keith Waterhouse rewrote *Diary of a Nobody* from the point of view of the wife – he called it *Mrs Pooter's Diary*.

It's important to choose old stories that you can expect your audience to be familiar with. Most of us know about *Red Riding Hood*, very few of us know the *Saga of Erik the Red*.

## Things to remember

▶ Write out anything that's nagging at you.

▶ Learn to be anarchic, break down taboos and think outside the box.

▶ Get in touch with your inner child.

▶ Use free-thinking and lists to generate ideas.

▶ Once you have ideas, use discipline, rewrite and polish.

▶ Don't polish until you've finished the first draft.

▶ Ideas for comedy are all around you.

# 4

## Language

In this chapter you will learn:
- *about working with words*
- *about the rhythms of language*
- *about word pictures.*

Comedy writing is all about words. You may be seeing hysterically funny pictures in your head, but unless you can put them into words no one will ever know.

The language you choose to use, both vocabulary and grammar, will affect both the style and the content of your work. You can write:

> *Dear Sir or Madam, It has come to my attention that you are in arrears.*

or:

> *Hi, I just remembered you owe me some dough.*

The content is the same, but the style is entirely different. In many areas of life we're inclined to be rather dismissive of style ('all style and no substance') but in writing, style is absolutely crucial. If the style is wrong in some way, then the content simply won't be communicated. And in the case of comedy, style is a large part of what makes people laugh. Neither of the sentences above is funny in itself, but you might be heading for a laugh if the first one was a note a mother put in her child's sandwiches, and the second one was a letter from a Bank Manager trying to be customer friendly.

## A sense of rhythm

There is a rhythm to all language, and comedy has its own rhythm, or rather rhythms. Some writers have a natural feel for this, but others have to learn it. It's difficult to teach someone a feeling for rhythm, but you can learn it by absorbing comedy writing and then imitating. Out of this process you'll eventually develop your own rhythm. Reading your work out loud will give you a feel for its rhythm.

Here's an American joke:

> *A man dreamt he was a muffler on a car, and then he turned into part of a wheel. He woke up exhausted and tired.*

The rhythm of this feels all wrong to me, because we'd normally say 'tired and exhausted'. So I'd want to rewrite the joke:

> *A man dreamt he was part of a car wheel, and then he turned into a muffler. He woke up tired and exhausted.*

You'll also need to be sensitive to the type of language used by your audience. The American joke doesn't work for the UK since we don't use the word 'muffler'. So here it is rewritten for the UK:

> *A man dreamt he was part of a car wheel, and then he turned into an exhaust. He woke up tired and exhausted.*

And there's the joke ruined, because the word 'exhaust' in the first sentence anticipates the punchline and gives it away. This joke doesn't travel.

Rhythm in performance can be quite different from rhythm on the page. Most performers have their own way of pacing a joke and audiences learn to tell when the punchline is due. A pause just before it is the most common way:

> *I do like children* (pause) *but I couldn't eat a whole one.*

The pause makes it obvious the punchline is next but there are different rhythms to an afterthought. It can either be added quickly, before the audience expects it, or after a longer pause when they should have assumed that joke was finished and the next one was on its way:

> *I do like children (pause) but I couldn't eat a whole one. (long pause) It's different if they're chocolate coated, obviously.*

On the page the writer creates rhythm through sentence structure and punctuation. Although people vary, mostly we don't read one word at a time and are vaguely aware, as we read, of the next few words ahead of us. If you simply substitute a comma for the pause, then the reader will get to the punchline almost before they realize it. This is fine for a joke book, but in continuous prose (novels or journalism) you might want to pace the laugh with a few extra words:

> *I do like children, truly I do, it's just that I couldn't eat a whole one.*

You can add afterthoughts or play with the joke:

> *He had an expression on his face like someone who, after trotting out his favourite joke that he liked children but couldn't eat a whole one, finds himself offered a plate of tiny chocolate coated body parts.*

---

**Comedy insight – MIRANDA HART**
*Watch, read, learn and absorb from comedy new and old, but don't lose your distinctive voice.*

Miranda Hart is a comedy actress and writer

---

## Word pictures

One of the basic tenets of writing is 'show don't tell'. With descriptive writing this means don't simply state the facts. Don't say 'he had an odd-shaped head' because that won't make anyone laugh – there's no funny picture. Instead look for an image – maybe say 'he had a head shaped like a rugby ball'. This creates a picture in the minds of your audience, which you can embellish as much as you like: 'he had a head shaped like a rugby ball after an All-Blacks game – a bit battered and the stitching was coming loose'.

Dickens is the past master of this type of description. Since he was paid by the word he wasn't interested in economy but even so he could sum up a character's appearance in a few words. Here is Mrs Pipchin in *Dombey & Son*:

> *This celebrated Mrs Pipchin was a marvellous ill-favoured, ill-conditioned old lady, of a stooping figure, with a mottled face, like bad marble, a hook nose, and a hard grey eye, that looked as if it might have been hammered at on an anvil without sustaining any injury.*

Of course the image of the anvil isn't just amusing, it conveys her personality as well. And note that the description builds towards the end, which is both the funniest and the most important part.

Dickens can also do this without using imagery, as in this description of Mr Murdstone's sister in *David Copperfield*:

> *A gloomy-looking lady she was; dark, like her brother, whom she greatly resembled in face and voice; and with very heavy eyebrows, nearly meeting over her large nose, as if, being disabled by the wrongs of her sex from wearing whiskers, she had carried them to that account.*

EXERCISE

### Exercise

Describe someone's appearance briefly and in a comedic way. You can use yourself, someone you know, a celebrity or a fictional character.

### ADJECTIVES AND ADVERBS

These descriptive words are a two-edged weapon for any writer. Too many of them and your writing will lack focus, too few and it will read like a report. One common piece of advice given to writers is to remove all the adverbs and adjectives from an early draft, and only replace the ones that are absolutely essential. Of course this has a profound effect on the rhythm.

Dickens, with his financial need for a high word count, tended to sprinkle descriptive words about liberally. It's interesting to look at the two descriptions with most of them taken out:

> *This Mrs Pipchin was an old lady, with a face like marble, a hook nose, and a grey eye, that looked as if it might have been hammered at on an anvil without sustaining any injury.*

*She was like her brother, whom she resembled in face and voice; and with eyebrows nearly meeting over her nose, as if, being disabled by the wrongs of her sex from wearing whiskers, she had carried them to that account.*

Which do you prefer? For me, Mrs Pipchin reads better without her modifiers, and Murdstone's sister is happier with them.

### USING LISTS

We've already seen how the rule of three works. You can also use longer lists for comedy effect. Here's Jane Austen listing characteristics in a letter to her sister in 1800 – and note the rhythm of the second sentence:

*Mrs Blount was the only one much admired. She appeared exactly as she did in September, with the same broad face, diamond bandeau, white shoes, pink husband, and fat neck.*

P. G. Wodehouse created a much longer list to describe someone overdoing the solicitude in *Lord Emsworth Acts for the Best*, with the funniest item at the end (and incidentally, 'muffler' used in the English sense):

*But when the fellow did the same thing day after day, night after night, every time he caught him sitting; when he offered him an arm to help him across floors; when he assisted him up stairs, along corridors, down paths, out of rooms and into raincoats; when he snatched objects from his hands to carry them himself; when he came galloping out of the house on dewy evenings laden down with rugs, mufflers, hats and, on one occasion, positively, a blasted respirator … why, then Lord Emsworth's proud spirit rebelled.*

Exercise

Use a list to describe someone. You can use yourself, someone you know, a celebrity or a fictional character.

**Author insight**
A great example of the power of anarchic thinking is Jonathan Swift's *A Modest Proposal*, in which he suggests that famine can be solved by people eating their own babies. Try reading this, or Daphne du Maurier's short story *The Way of the Cross* – this isn't a comedy, but it does show a writer using anarchic thinking.

### IDIOMS

Idioms are ways of using language that are not literally true but which everyone understands, such as 'rule of thumb' meaning 'rough estimate'. Sometimes the meaning could just about be figured out by an alien with a dictionary, such as 'get over it', but the most useful to the comedy writer are the ones with no literal connection to the meaning they convey, such as 'fine kettle of fish' meaning 'a mess or a muddle'. Other idioms are more subtle, for instance 'don't start anything' means 'don't start trouble'.

You can get laughs from playing around with idioms. For example:

> **Some jump leads went into a bar and asked for beer. The barman said 'alright, but just don't start anything'.**

And here's a Wodehouse example from *The Inimitable Jeeves*:

> *'Warm-hearted! I should think he has to wear asbestos vests...'*

Alternatively you can turn idioms upside down: 'pure as the driven snow' can become 'pure as the driven slush'. This works best if the idiom is also a cliché.

### CLICHÉS, APHORISMS AND PROVERBS

Clichés, aphorisms and proverbs can be used in similar ways to idioms. Oscar Wilde took 'nothing succeeds like success' and turned it into 'nothing succeeds like excess'. Very witty, unlike the very silly version 'nothing succeeds (sucks seeds) like a parrot with no teeth'.

You'll have more chances to practise this kind of joke writing in Chapter 5.

### CATCHPHRASES

A catchphrase is a phrase repeated so often that it becomes associated with that performer or show. They've been documented back into the 16th century and no doubt go back further than that. They're not usually funny as such, but become so through repetition. In a vote on the most popular TV catchphrases Victor Meldrew's 'I don't believe it' was the winner – this is only funny in context. Stand-up comedians often have a catchphrase and *The Fast Show* allocated a catchphrase to almost every series of sketches.

### ACCENTS AND REGIONAL SPEECH

There's a lot of comedy value in accents, but you need to know what you're doing. It's best to stick with accents that you know well and can hear in your head as you write. If you're writing for a specific performer you'll know what they can and can't manage, but if you're writing a script without knowing who will perform it, then only specify an accent if it's absolutely essential. You don't want your script rejected on the grounds that it's too difficult to cast.

Most accents are part of a larger regional speech, and so there's an associated rhythm, grammar and vocabulary. A Cockney character might say 'Me ol' woman give us a right ear-bashing' and you clearly should not write that as 'My wife gave me quite a telling off'. Some slangy words are so well known that you can assume readers and performers will recognize them, so you can use them rather than the correct form – 'innit' for 'isn't it' is a good example.

Representing accents on the page is a minefield. In a script it's best to mention the accent required at the beginning and then spell the words normally. So for the Cockney character, specify Cockney in the character notes and write 'My old woman give us a right ear-bashing.' This retains the vocabulary and grammatical peculiarities while still being perfectly readable.

It's slightly more problematic for prose writers, who need to give a flavour of the accent for every speech without cluttering the page up with punctuation and semi-phonetic spellings. Arnold Bennett got it about right in *The Card*:

> *'Ye're here for th' better part o' some time, then,' observed Mrs Hullins, looking facts in the face. 'I've told you about my son Jack. He's been playing six weeks. He starts to-day, and he'll gi'me summat Saturday.'*

Whatever you do avoid the knots D. H. Lawrence managed to tie himself into. Stuff like this from *Lady Chatterley's Lover* is beyond parody:

> *'Why,' he began, in the broad slow dialect. 'Your Ladyship's as welcome as Christmas ter th' hut an' th' key an' iverythink as is. On'y this time O' th' year ther's bods ter set, an' Ah've got ter be potterin' abaht a good bit, seein' after 'em, an' a'. Winter time Ah ned 'ardly come nigh th' pleece. But what wi' spring, an' Sir Clifford wantin' ter start th' pheasants... An' your Ladyship'd non want me tinkerin' around an' about when she was 'ere, all the time.'*

## Things to remember

▶ Style is as important as content.

▶ Language has its own rhythms.

▶ Show don't tell.

▶ Be disciplined with adjectives and adverbs.

▶ Use lists to build to a laugh.

▶ Play around with idioms, clichés, aphorisms and proverbs.

▶ Take care with accents and dialects.

# 5

# Jokes

In this chapter you will learn:
- *about writing short jokes*
- *about editing jokes to improve them*
- *about longer jokes.*

---
**Comedy insight – CHRIS RITCHIE**

*The most common mistake that new comedy writers make is writing a sitcom before they know how to write jokes. I get people applying to the comedy degree I run who tell me they have written a sitcom and they haven't even done stand-up (you don't have to, but it sure helps!). You have to start small. One-liners, then a monologue, then expand into sketches. Also, no one is going to buy a sitcom cold like that. You have to work your way up or else it is waste of labour (unless you see it as practising writing). Placing work is hard but there are ways of getting it on somewhere. Try writing spec scripts as well. Also writers perform stand-up – people like Rob Grant, Stephen Merchant and Robin Ince are on the circuit and approachable. Talk to them. They know what they're on about.*

Chris Ritchie created the innovative Comedy: Writing & Performance degree at
Southampton Solent University in 2006 and is the editor of *Comedy Studies*

---

Many aspiring comedy writers are rather dismissive of joke writing, probably because they remember the traditional style of stand-up that consisted of a series of quickfire jokes around a single topic. Eventually this format became rather tired and observational comedy, which is more about pointing out the oddities of real life, replaced it. In fact many observational routines do include a few jokes. The wheel always turns and joke-based stand-up, which never entirely went away, is staging something of a revival.

In any case jokes are the most basic comedy unit and joke writing is an important skill that exercises your comedy muscles.

Jokes are short, self-contained nuggets of humour and in their most basic form consist of just a set-up and punchline:

>*Set-up: A horse went into a bar.*
>
>*Punchline: The barman said 'why the long face?'*

The set-up should include all the information you need to understand the punchline without giving it away. In this example, just the fact that it's a horse is enough information. Because it's a formulaic joke the audience will know at once that the punchline will be something to do with a horse's characteristics, but, unless they've heard it before, they won't guess what. It's the surprise of the twisted logic that creates the laugh.

Single jokes can be extended with afterthoughts to form part of a routine:

>*A white horse went into a bar.*
>*The barman said 'why the long face?'*
>*The horse started coughing.*
>*The barman said 'you need to be in the horspital'*
>*The horse said 'shut up and gimme a brandy'*
>*The barman said 'you know we have a whisky named after you'*
>*The horse said 'what, Sebastian?'*

Single-frame cartoons are usually based around a joke. The drawing is the set-up and the caption is the punchline.

---

## Writing jokes

Like any skill your joke writing will improve with practice, so try to write 20 jokes a day. Don't worry about the quality at this stage, the aim is to produce quantity and edit out the poor ones later on, before you submit them anywhere. And as you keep working at it you'll find your standards gradually rising. At first you'll only think of the obvious jokes, but as you already know, persistence pays. After doing a few, say five or six, you'll find yourself trying that bit harder and reaching that bit higher.

## Exercise

To get you started, here's an exercise bank of 14 different joke writing exercises with explanations and draft examples. Work through them in order, over several days if need be. Just like going to the gym, you'll get better at it the more you do it.

### 1 ADJECTIVES

Make a list of 20 adjectives. Now choose one of them – go for one that is simple and specific, such as 'green'. Make a list of everything you can think of connected with green. You might end up with something like this:

> *Green light, green for go, Green Line bus, green green grass of home, little green men, green card, Greenpeace, green fees, green tea, green with envy, greenhouse, village green, greenhouse gases, climate change, frogs, apples, cabbage and other vegetables, vegetarianism.*

There are more, but you get the idea. Now look for simple jokes using the list, for instance:

> *When I was a teenager I had a terrible weight problem. I didn't just have puppy fat: when we were on holiday, if I sunbathed on the beach, Greenpeace would send a crew to try and re-float me.*

> *What kind of frog is green and dangerous? One with a machine gun.*

If you can't manage 20 jokes from one adjective, repeat the process with others.

### 2 LOOK FOR OPPOSITES

Using an adjective from your list, write down as many opposites as you can think of.

Sticking with green, you might get:

> *Red, stop, pollution, climate change denial, driving an SUV, carnivorism, and so on.*

Now look for the jokes around the opposites, for instance:

> *My doctor told me to eat more greens, so last night I had a steak. Cows eat grass don't they?*

### 3 EVERYDAY ITEMS

Make a list of 20 everyday items, things that we all use. Don't look for funny items, in fact the more mundane the better. Now seek out alternative uses for each one, for instance:

> *Vodka: use vodka to clean jewellery, polish a chandelier, remove lipstick from clothing, clean greenfly off house plants.*

And then look for the jokes:

> *I read somewhere you can use vodka to get lipstick off your collar, so I drank half a bottle – I couldn't see the lipstick but my wife could. Next time I'll get her to drink the vodka.*

> *Don't use vodka to clean greenfly off house plants. They'll just throw a party and invite all the other bugs.*

### 4 GET VISUAL

Cut out 20 photos from magazines, the quirkier the better. Write funny captions for each one. For instance, a photo of two celebrities on the red carpet might be captioned with the shorter one saying 'I can see right up your nose'.

### 5 DRAWING

Now move on to creating your own visuals. It doesn't matter if you can't draw, you can use stick people, flowers, or even geometric shapes. For instance, you could draw two identical flowers with the caption 'There's something I really like about you'. Or flowers looking up at a leafy tree with the caption 'He won't be so full of it come the autumn'.

### 6 CLICHÉS AND PROVERBS

Make a list of 20 clichés or proverbs. Now play with each one and rearrange it in some way, for instance:

> *Been there, done that, got the T-shirt, worn it and turned it into dusters.*

*People who live in glass houses shouldn't leave the curtains open at bath time.*

### 7 ADD-ONS

Now try to rewrite each cliché or proverb with an add-on to undermine it. For instance 'money can't buy you happiness' could be turned into:

*Money can't buy you happiness, but it makes the kids stay in touch.*

### 8 REVERSING

Go through your cliché/proverb list again and find a reverse:

*If money can't buy you happiness, then why do we pay for chocolate?*

### 9 DEFINITIONS

Make a list of 20 abstract nouns and write alternative definitions for each one. There are two ways of doing this. The first way is to play with the meaning of the word and come up with another meaning that reveals a truth:

*Experience: the name people give to their mistakes.*

The other way is to ignore the correct meaning and find another based on the sound of the word:

*Negligent: absentmindedly answering the front door in your nightie.*

### 10 ODDITIES

Look down your various lists and randomly pair off items, then make a joke from the pairing. Let's say our pair is tennis rackets and toasters:

*My toaster shoots the toast into the air. Still if I catch it with my tennis racket I get instant croutons.*

### 11 LIGHTBULB JOKES

Make a list of 20 groups of people (by profession or hobby) and write lightbulb jokes for them.

*Q How many computer programmers does it take to change a lightbulb?*

A Only one, but why bother, the light socket will be obsolete in six months anyway.

### 12 FUNNY NAMES

Use your list of groups to create funny names relevant to the group, for instance:

*Librarians: Otto Biographie, Allison Wonderland*

Sometimes these are funnier presented in two stages:

*Mr and Mrs Wallcarpet, and their son, Walter Wallcarpet.*

### 13 READ THE NEWS

Buy a newspaper and use the contents to create at least 20 jokes. Headline items will produce jokes with a short shelf life, but there is a demand for them. The real comedy gold is in the inside pages and small news items. Scientists and researchers are particularly fruitful:

*Research has shown that a teenager costs thousands of pounds – but why would anybody want to buy one?*

*Researchers who discovered that the smell of roses and chocolates induce romantic feelings have been unable to account for the popularity of diamond rings.*

### 14 GET PERSONAL

Look through all your lists and write 20 insults.

*My ex believed that money can't buy you happiness, which is why he never spent any money on me.*

*He has a mind like a steel trap – always closed.*

**Author insight**
The very first joke I sold was for radio, a spoof news item that was just over 100 words. They rewrote it and broadcast 60 words. I was very lucky to sell it and I never made that mistake again.

## Editing jokes

Once you've written your first batch of 20 jokes leave them for a day or so and then start editing them – but remember, don't throw anything away. Even a weak joke might be useful one day as part of a build-up to a bigger laugh, or you might see a way of improving it. So when you edit out the worst jokes, rather than delete them, put them in a Bad Jokes folder.

Before you start work there are a few key things to remember:

**Be economical with words.** In a short joke, every word has to earn its keep, for instance, the Greenpeace joke is much improved by being shortened:

> *I didn't just have puppy fat: when I sunbathed on the beach, Greenpeace would try to re-float me.*

**Keep the best till last.** Make sure the laugh is on the last word, for instance:

> *If money can't buy happiness, then why isn't chocolate free?*

**Don't reveal the punchline in the set-up** – this is usually a question of avoiding one key word, for instance removing 'frog' from my earlier set-up gives this:

> *What's green and dangerous? A frog with a machine gun.*

**Use specific vocabulary.** Don't say 'dog', say 'poodle' or 'Doberman' – it helps create the picture, for instance:

> *My ex believed that money can't buy you happiness, which is why I never had an engagement ring.*

**Don't be too direct.** If you say 'he looked like a vicar', it won't get a laugh, but you might get a small laugh from:

> *I took one look at him and booked him for my son's christening.*

---

## Longer jokes

Longer jokes are more like a funny short story:

> *A farmer was showing a visitor round his farm. When they got to the pigsty, the visitor noticed one of the pigs had a wooden leg. 'Poor thing' he said to the farmer, 'how did that happen?' 'Ah,' said the farmer, 'that's a very special pig that is. One night we were all asleep in the farmhouse and a spark from the fire set the house alight. The pig could smell the burning so he jumped out of the sty, ran to the house,*

*broke in through a window, ran upstairs and dragged me
out of bed. Then he went back into the burning house and
rescued the rest of the family. He even got the dog and the
budgie out. Yes sire, that's quite a special pig.' 'Amazing,'
said the visitor, 'but how did he get the wooden leg?' 'Oh
come on,' said the farmer, 'you can't eat a pig like that all
in one go.'*

As you can see, there are no laughs along the way in a joke of
this sort. It all hangs on the punchline and it's just as likely to
be greeted with a groan as a laugh. These are jokes for telling
to friends rather than in a professional context – not many
paying audiences will wait that long for a laugh. Ronnie Corbett
developed a technique for telling a long joke by using constant
asides to raise small laughs before the big one at the end, rather
like this:

*A farmer was showing a visitor round his farm. Well, I say
farm, it was more like a factory with animals. Not that they
minded though – you should've seen those chickens queuing up
to clock in. So anyway, when they got to the pigsty…*

A professional comedy writer would also see at once that the joke
needs to be more specific:

*My cousin had a mid-life crisis. He left his highly stressful job
as an estate agent, I mean you know how difficult it can be
measuring rooms, and he bought a farm. So I went to visit him
one day…*

### WRITING A LONG JOKE

This is often about finding an anecdote to fit a punchline, since most
of the length of the joke is in the set-up. You can see that the farmer
joke could have taken any number of routes to get to the punchline.
Try to construct a route that appears to be leading off in quite a
different direction so that the surprise at the end is as big as possible,
because the audience has had to wait for it. The route chosen for
the farmer joke points the audience at the fire, which distracts them
before suddenly introducing the idea that the pig lost his leg during
the rescue.

Avoid any key words and concepts in the body of the joke. Don't, for instance, do this:

> **When they got to the pigsty, the visitor noticed one of the pigs had a wooden leg. He said 'what a shame, one less roasting joint off that one'.**

Look through the jokes you've already written, choose one of the punchlines and write a long joke for it. If none of them seem suitable then use this punning punchline: What's this left ear/left 'ere?

### RUNNING JOKES

A running joke is a joke that's repeated, with variations, through a piece of writing. The classic comedy movie *Airplane* was stuffed with running gags, from 'don't call me Shirley' (every time someone starts a sentence 'surely') to Ted Striker's 'drink problem' (he misses his mouth every time).

Running jokes can be used in any kind of comedy writing. Here's a small example from *The Inimitable Jeeves* which starts:

> **The brother was a small round cove with a face rather like a sheep.**

and a couple of pages later:

> **…and as for the brother, he looked like a sheep with a secret sorrow.**

> **At this point the brother … gave a little cough, like a sheep caught in the mist on a mountain top.**

### THEMED JOKES

As well as taking a single joke and repeating it with variations, you can run a series of themed jokes through a piece. These are particularly useful in diary format novels where they create a feeling of continuity. For instance in *The Secret Diary of Adrian Mole aged 13¾* Adrian repeatedly writes to the BBC and in *The Timewaster Diaries* Robin's wife Rita is constantly spraining her ankle.

## Things to remember

▶ Joke writing is a good way to develop your skills.

▶ Don't give up too soon.

▶ Write 20 jokes a day.

▶ Use lists to generate joke ideas.

▶ Edit the jokes after a break.

▶ Be economical and specific.

▶ Don't give the punchline away in the set-up.

▶ Longer jokes must have a surprising punchline.

▶ Running jokes are repeated with variations.

# 6

# Stand-up

In this chapter you will learn:
- *about stand-up comedy*
- *about traditional and observational stand-up*
- *about routining.*

Stand-up is just what it sounds like – you stand up in front of an audience and make them laugh. As a writer you have to decide whether to perform your own jokes or whether to work with a performer. Whichever method you choose, it's very important to get your routines in front of an audience to test them out. Even if you don't see yourself as a performer, you'll learn a lot if you have a go.

Don't be afraid of the audience. They've turned up with the intention of enjoying themselves. They want to laugh, so they'll usually meet you more than halfway. Think about their concerns, their attitude to things when you're writing. This doesn't have to be about agreeing with or endorsing their attitude, it's much more about understanding it.

........................................................................................
**Author insight**

If you're nervous about performing, a prop might help – for instance a guitar round your neck gives you somewhere to rest your hands.
........................................................................................

Exercise

Go to a live stand-up performance. Observe the audience and work out how the comic establishes a connection with them. At a pinch you can do this exercise by watching a recording at home.

Some themes are universal. You can talk to any audience about old age, although you'd take a different perspective for teenagers compared with pensioners. Other themes are very specific. If the routine is for an audience of estate agents or cacti enthusiasts, then you can do jokes that only they would understand. You'd also need to do your research too of course.

Next, think about the performer, which means think about their on-stage character. Make contact with a stand-up who works locally, so that you can watch them performing. Try to meet them and learn as much as possible about their take on comedy. Ask who their comedy heroes are, and what inspires them. Make sure you understand how they like to open and close their routines and how they like to deal with hecklers.

Exercise

Watch a recording of a stand-up routine. Work out how it develops and moves from laugh to laugh.

---

## The basics of routining

When you're assembling a stand-up routine aim for two or three laughs a minute – they won't all be big belly laughs. Start with something simple that doesn't require much of a set-up, so that the comic can get that all-important first laugh. It helps to choose something that the audience can connect with – it gets them on the comic's side. Later on the routine can become more fantastical or surreal, but not with the opening gags. The last few laughs of a routine are the most important ones, as that's what the audience will remember afterwards.

Choose an order for your routine – it can be chronological (e.g. from wedding to honeymoon) or anything else that makes sense.

Don't have similar types of joke too close together and look at the pacing. Try to identify where the big laughs will fall and have smaller laughs either side to create peaks and troughs. Always save the best joke and the biggest laugh for the end. Judging the size of the laughs isn't easy, but you'll learn a lot when you see the routine performed, or perform it yourself. Always be prepared to rewrite the next day.

### GO WITH THE FLOW

There are ways of keeping the routine flowing. You can link groups of jokes on disparate topics by writing a joke that connects them. The more subtly you do this, the more spontaneous the routine will seem.

Reincorporation means mentioning something early on, moving on from it and then returning to it towards the end when the audience has forgotten about it. It can generate huge laughs if it's done well.

Early jokes can be used to set up the later ones, perhaps by establishing certain characteristics. For instance the joke about eating steak to get more greens could be used to establish that the comic isn't into healthy eating, and it could lead on to jokes about environmental matters or political correctness, always with the comic going the unfashionable route.

---

**Comedy insight – KEV F SUTHERLAND**

*Many many scripts entered into* **The Sitcom Trials** *consist of talking heads wittering on, discussing events that happened in the past. This is rarely interesting. Conversely, that is all stand-up is, so you have to learn the difference between the disciplines.*

Kev F Sutherland is a comedian and comic artist (*Beano, Marvel, Viz,* etc.)

---

## Traditional stand-up

Traditional stand-up routines are joke based. Some comics just tell one joke after another, while others pace the jokes with fillers.

### WRITING A TRADITIONAL ROUTINE

If you've already generated a heap of jokes, you might well have the makings of a routine. Some of the examples from the Jokes chapter (Chapter 5) can be turned into a short routine even though they weren't written with that intention:

> *When I was a teenager I had a terrible weight problem. I didn't just have puppy fat: if I sunbathed on the beach Greenpeace would send a crew to try and re-float me. Still, I did manage to find a husband. He was quite a guy. He had a mind like a steel trap – always closed. And boy, was he mean. Never spent*

*a penny if he could avoid it. Well he believed that money can't buy you happiness. I said to him, oh yeah? If money can't buy you happiness, then how come we have to pay for chocolate?*

At the beginning this needs more jokes, either about puppy fat or other aspects of teenage angst. When it moves on to the mean husband it looks more promising, and could lead to a rant about marriage or maybe a series of money jokes.

### Exercise

**Take some of the jokes you've already written and create a short routine.**

Another way to create a traditional routine is to choose a topic and make a list of items connected with the topic. Take each item and break it down into subheadings. Then use the techniques you've already learnt to generate jokes. Once you've produced a lot of jokes, many more than you need, then choose the best three from each group. When you assemble the routine, keep the jokes from each topic together, saving the best for last each time.

Traditional comics often have a set format for their opening – for years Ken Dodd has used 'What a lovely day? What a lovely day for...' A lot of traditional comics also like to finish with a song, a piece of advice or homespun philosophy.

## Observational stand-up

**Comedy insight – TONY STAVEACRE**

*Don't shy away from including some jokes. A lot of comedy today is the comedy of embarrassment. If there is an audience, they are likely to be sitting there silently with mouths gaping open at the awfulness of the situation in which today's comedy heroes find themselves. But jokes are ok. And nothing is more satisfying for the comedy writer than to be standing at the back of the studio or theatre and to hear the glorious sound of laughter. 'I made them laugh...!' Put it on your tombstone.*

Tony Staveacre is a writer/producer in TV, radio and theatre

Writing a routine for an observational comic requires a different technique because it's based on observing the quirks of life that we all share but haven't necessarily noticed. Observations like this connect the comic with the audience and produce the kind of laughter that is more like a groan of recognition. The real belly laughs come from playing with the observation, taking it beyond reality to madness or fantasy.

One obvious potential problem is that professional comedians quite quickly find that they don't share much with their audience. Working at night, sleeping during the day, on the road many weeks of the year – this is not a typical lifestyle. Some years ago Jasper Carrott built an entire routine around the fact that his increasing affluence was changing his relationship with his audience, but it would soon get tiresome if everyone did this. As a writer, you may be able to help the performer stay in touch with normality.

### WRITING AN OBSERVATIONAL ROUTINE

The first step is to make the observations. You can do these at random, for instance:

> *When men are watching TV, they can't hear you talk to them.*
>
> *If you want to stop your computer, click Start.*
>
> *Dogs have to pee every 30 seconds on a walk.*
>
> *Men like to rearrange the dishes in the dishwasher.*

Or you can choose a topic and see how many observations you can make round it:

> *Dogs have to pee every 30 seconds on a walk.*
>
> *The nastier the dog, the more likely the owner is to say 'that's just his way of being friendly'.*
>
> *Sometimes his way of being friendly is to hump your leg.*
>
> *People who kiss their dogs on the mouth never seem to realize that the last thing the dog kissed was another dog's bottom.*

Exercise

Write down your own observations.

Look through the observations and see what catches your eye. Let's start with the first one about men watching TV. Make notes around the topic:

> *Men – can't scratch their heads and eat a boiled egg at the same time. Can't talk while they're watching TV.*
>
> *Multitasking has been in the news, because research has shown that women actually are better at it.*
>
> *When kids do their homework in front of the TV are they multitasking?*
>
> *Women multitasking – cooking, cleaning, helping with homework, soothing the baby and holding down a career. Shopping lists, booking holidays, ferrying kids to ballet and football. Putting on make-up at the traffic lights, ordering groceries online in the lunch hour.*
>
> *What about jobs that men used to do – cutting the grass, servicing machinery or changing a tap washer? Do they still do them?*

EXERCISE

Exercise

Choose one of your observations and expand it.

Next make choices, based on the audience and the performer. Let's say that this set is for a comic who uses the voice of an older woman, a man-hating cleaning lady with a lazy husband. She doesn't have a career, and has grown-up kids. The audience is likely to be in the same age group, so we need to edit out any topics that don't fit.

EXERCISE

Exercise

Decide what sort of audience and performer you're writing for (real or imagined) and edit your notes accordingly.

The next task is to arrange an order:

*Introduce multitasking – new scientific research.*

*Talk about it in a fairly realistic way – things women can do which men can't do.*

*Extend into the realms of fantasy – a woman still multitasking while having sex.*

Put your notes into order.

Finally, write it up. This routine is for a clearly defined comedy character with a specific voice which has to be taken into consideration. Then edit, rewrite and maybe end up with this:

*I've got nothing against men, mind, but I seen in the papers, them scientists has worked out that men can only do one thing at a time while women, right, women are what's called multifunctional.*

*Now what that means is a woman can cook the breakfast, delouse the dog, change the spark plug on the motor mower and do the kids' homework all at the same time. But men can only do one thing. And if he's scratching his head, well don't expect him to do nothing else. Blimey we didn't need no scientist to tell us that did we? I think we'd worked that one out hadn't we girls.*

*And I don't want to go on about sex, I leave that to the Women's Institute, but you know what it's like don't you, you've got the man shouting yes yes, while the women is getting on with her orgasm, writing a shopping list, and trying to decide whether to go to Venice or Venezuela for next year's holiday. Oh, and if it's Monday morning she's probably changing the sheets and if it's Saturday she'll be stripping the wallpaper off with a chisel, ready to start decorating.*

**Write a short routine based on your observations.**

As we've already seen, with joke-based stand-up you aim for three jokes on a topic, and the same concept applies to observational stand-up. In other words, that was enough about multitasking – time to move on to the next topic, which in this case was triggered by a news item about mapping the Human Genome. The same process of making notes and choosing an order produces these opening remarks on the topic:

> *I seen on the Internet that them scientists have mapped the Genome. I can see you're surprised I use the Internet. Well, I am one of them silver sufferers. You see it's us women what are into this hands-on technology. Men buy the computers, right, and they boast about the size of their rams and hard drives or whatever, but it's us women what work out how to use 'em. I tell you I roar down that information superhighway so fast it's a wonder I haven't been booked for speeding.*

With one more topic – holidays – the process can be repeated to produce a short set. An entry level set for a comedy club is three to five minutes so aim for that to start with. Longer sets are ten or twenty minutes which is more of a writing challenge – it doesn't work if you just pad out a short set.

**Repeat the process with two more topics.**

In fact this set was written for a real performer, who was able to test it on a willing group and it was immediately obvious that links were needed between the topics. For instance, the link between multitasking and the Human Genome went like this:

> *And talking of chisels – don't men ever go mad if you use one instead of a screwdriver? I mean what's the big deal, they look*

*the same don't they? Anyway I was only scraping out the oven, no call for him making all that fuss.*

*'Course he still thinks that sort of thing is woman's work along with hoovering, gardening and servicing the car. So don't give me all that New Man stuff. He says he done his bit when he wrote the cheque for the dishwasher. So why is it that as fast as I put the plates in he takes 'em out again and just ever so slightly rearranges them? What's that all about then?*

*Of course we're told it's all in the genes...*

Exercise

Create links between your topics so that your routine has flow.

### DOUBLE ACTS

A traditional double act consists of a straight person and a funny person, usually men of course. Morecambe and Wise took this to its peak, and recently it's all but disappeared. Double acts now are more likely to consist of multi-talented performers who adopt a range of characters, so that writing for them is mainly about sketch writing. If you're interested in writing for a ventriloquist, treat it like a double act.

### IMPRESSIONISTS

Impressionists need scripts that are funny, sharp and in character, or rather characters. You'll need an understanding of the performer's talents and limitations and an insight into the subjects of the impressions.

## Things to remember

▶ You'll have greater insight if you try stand-up yourself.

▶ Stand-up comedians have on-stage characters.

▶ Create both big and small laughs.

- ▶ The last few laughs are the most important.

- ▶ Have an underlying logic to the order of a routine.

- ▶ Observational routines start with quirky observations rather than jokes.

- ▶ Three laughs from a topic is about right.

- ▶ Insert links between topics.

# 7

## Simple characters and situations

In this chapter you will learn:
- *that character is important*
- *that characters need conflict*
- *that sources for characters are all around you*
- *about comedy situations.*

---

**Comedy insight – ERIC CHAPPELL**
*Always remember that character comes first and situation comes second.*

Eric Chappell is a writer

---

Once you move beyond writing jokes you'll find that character underpins every aspect of comedy writing. You've already seen that the on-stage character of a stand-up comic has a direct bearing on the type of routine that will work for them. Stand-up is not a question of getting up on stage and just being yourself, although most stand-ups are an exaggerated version of themselves. A smaller number of stand-ups create an entire fictional character – who would think that ignorant bigoted Al Murray, the pub landlord, was in reality Oxford-educated Alastair Murray?

If you're writing for either type of stand-up, you'll need to constantly check that you're staying within the boundaries of their on-stage character. If you work with someone who's at the start of their career, then you may be able to help them develop that character.

Exercise

Take one of your earlier jokes and rewrite it in the style of your favourite stand-up. Now rewrite it for your least favourite stand-up.

It's similar if you're writing a humorous article for a magazine or writing a first person short story or novel. The voice that you use will either be an exaggeration of your normal voice, or else you'll create an entirely new character and write in their voice.

Here's me using a version of my own voice for an article about why I bought a motorcaravan:

> *When I first met Mike it was winter time and everything looked perfect. We agreed about all the important things in life – money, politics, and how to spend your holidays – camping of course.*
>
> *Come the spring, I, as usual, put my tent up in the garden to air it, and that's when the trouble started. 'I hate frame tents,' Mike declared, rummaging in a carrier bag, 'we'll have to use this.' He threw onto the grass something that looked like scruffy faded orange handkerchief. 'No way,' I told him, 'am I sleeping in something a passing drunk might blow his nose on.'*

And here's me writing on the same topic using the voice of an invented posh totty character who is definitely nothing like me at all:

> *However many berths you have in your motoring caravan it is simply foolish to allow the butler to use one of them. The thing to do is to send the man on ahead with a pup tent, which will be quite adequate for his needs. With judicious planning it should be possible for him to serve one's breakfast at home and be on the camping site ready with luncheon just as one arrives.*

---

## Creating comedy characters

A lot of comedy uses very simple characters, often quite stereotypical, because they're easily recognized. Even the more unusual characters generally have a dominant characteristic that can be presented to the audience quickly and simply. Whether you're writing prose or for performance, the same guidelines apply to creating characters, although the ways you convey the information to your audience will differ. The most important thing is to give the character some sort of conflict.

There are three different levels of conflict and as a writer you can use any or all of them.

The first is inner conflict – a character who wants two different, and conflicting, things out of life. Basil Fawlty is a social climber who wants to mix with a better class of person, but he also wants to be affluent, and making money can be a grubby business.

The second is conflict with other people. In *Black Books* Bernard Black is at odds with everyone, including his two friends. A lot of comedy is written round the concept of a central, slightly odd, character who has no inner conflict but who is constantly in conflict with the people around them. Mr Pooter, the main character in *Diary of a Nobody*, is quite sure that he knows how life should be; his problem is that other people rarely agree with him. Mr Bean is a similar type of character.

These two types of conflict form the bulk of comedy within our culture, because most people can identify with them.

The third type of conflict is where the character is in conflict with society. This is clearly useful when a writer wants to make a political point and is more common in societies with high political tension. Tom Sharpe's novels *Indecent Exposure* and *Riotous Assembly* are about life in South Africa in the days of apartheid. He makes fun of all the races caught up in the regime, while also making the serious point that everyone is diminished by it.

In the UK we had *Citizen Smith*, a 1970s sitcom about a young left-winger who is at odds with the comfortable suburban life that surrounds him and who wants to start a revolution. However most of the comedy arises from his incompetence and inability to have any effect on the world he so dislikes.

## Stock characters

Stock characters are the ones we all recognize instantly: the tart with the heart of gold, the dithery vicar, the power-crazed traffic warden, and so on. Outside comedy they are generally thought to be undesirable and a sign of lazy writing, but in comedy they are extremely useful.

Jokes, quickies and sketches all rely heavily on stock characters because they are instantly recognizable and they behave in ways that the audience expects.

As a writer you have two choices. You can go with the stereotype and derive your comedy from exaggerating it beyond the expectations of the audience. Characters like Armstrong and Miller's Two Menopausal Ladies, with their violently exaggerated mood swings, fall into this category.

Alternatively you can undermine the expectation by having the character behave in the opposite way. This works very well, because the opposite way is bound to be incongruous – for instance, in the *Lumberjack Song* the Monty Python team created a manly looking lumberjack who yearned to wear women's underwear. More recently Catherine Tate's Nan Taylor is the opposite of what we'd expect from a grandmother.

Exercise

Make a list of ten stock characters and decide how you'd exaggerate and undermine each one.

## Character types

Only one step removed from stock characters, there are certain types that work particularly well in comedy and recur again and again. Stand-up comedians often base their persona on one of these basic comedy characters.

**The deadpan** Nothing but nothing will cause this character to bend a face muscle. Jack Dee has perfected this character.

**The fish out of water** ET and Crocodile Dundee are characters adrift in a strange culture. As well as comedy value, as they find their way around making mistakes due to their ignorance, they are also a good hook to hang a story on.

**The innocent** Often also a klutz (see later), but can be simply a childlike innocent constantly bewildered by his or her failures. These characters can also bring an offbeat perspective on the world, such as Father Dougal in *Father Ted*.

**The jester** A lot of stand-up comedians have taken the simple jester option in the past – Arthur Askey for instance – although the character is less popular in these cynical times.

**The klutz** A childlike character who keeps getting everything wrong – at first he can't get the lid off the ketchup, then it suddenly shoots off spraying him with red goo. He licks it off his clothing and ends up eating his tie. This works well in physical comedy, for example, Mr Bean.

**The know-it-all** At the opposite end of the spectrum from the innocent, this character is sure they know what's what. Del Boy in *Only Fools and Horses* is a good example. He has other, more lovable, qualities but that isn't essential, for instance David Brent in *The Office*.

**The loser** The loser is particularly popular in UK comedy – Tony Hancock developed the template for this on radio and TV. However it features in American movies too, for instance The Dude in *The Big Lebowski*.

**The neurotic** The neurotic worries about everything under the sun – Woody Allen has perfected this schtick.

**The social climber** The opposite of the vulgarian (see later), this character tries far too hard to be refined. Examples abound in class-obsessed UK comedy: Basil Fawlty, Hyacinth Bouquet, Harold Steptoe and so on.

**The vulgarian** This character pays no attention to social niceties or other people's needs. He takes the ketchup from the next table, returns it empty, helps himself to a chip from a child's plate and is chased down the road by the irate father. Example: both Rick and Eddy in *Bottom*.

---

# Sources for original characters

Characters need a spark of originality, and for that reason you should look all round you to find them, although no doubt you'll come to realize that most of the characters you create do fall into one of the character types mentioned earlier.

### PEOPLE WATCHING

If you observe people when you're out and about, you'll notice all sorts of interesting behaviours that may kick-start a character for you. Also look at people you already know.

Exercise

Write a brief description of a character you've observed in real life.

### PLAYS, MOVIES, TV, NOVELS

You will be influenced by the characters created by other writers; it's inevitable, although there's no excuse for shameless copying.

Exercise

Make a list of five serious characters from other writers' work and explore their comedy potential.

### REAL LIFE

There is plenty of comedy to be gained from writing about real life figures. If they are still alive or only recently dead you will have to consider legal aspects and the libel laws in particular. Historical figures though are fair game. You can either use the received wisdom about them (for instance, Henry VIII as both fat and cruel) or create entirely new characters for them.

Sue Limb created *The Wordsmiths at Gorsemere* for Radio 4 based around the lives of Wordsworth and Coleridge together with their families, friends and hangers on, many of whom are well known in their own right.

Exercise

Choose a real life figure and explore their comedy potential.

---

## Realism

A lot of comedy arises from exaggerating reality, and characters are no exception. However you have a choice in how far you take this. Ben Harper in *My Family* is a very slightly exaggerated character – I suspect most of us know someone who is quite a lot like him. Basil Fawlty is exaggerated, and yet many of us have been in hotels and restaurants that are not too far removed from Fawlty Towers. Douglas Reynholm, the boss of Reynholm Industries in *The IT Crowd*, is exaggerated beyond any connection with reality. Of course there are various kinds of realism – Bollo the talking gorilla in *The Mighty Boosh* is completely unreal in one sense, but has an instantly recognizable human character.

---

**Comedy insight – ANN GAWTHORPE**

*The most common mistake that new comedy writers make is making a character behave uncharacteristically just to get a laugh; there should be a good and logical reason for a character to behave outside their normal parameters.*

Ann Gawthorpe is a writer

---

## Characteristics

Characteristics are all the things that are on the surface of a character – how they look, move, speak and dress. In comedy writing they are very important and can generate a lot of laughs.

It's a good idea to visualize your characters physically. If you're writing for performance then you may find that an actor is cast who looks quite different from your mental image – accept that this happens, and if you're lucky the actor will take over and make the character live. While you're writing though, you need a picture in your head. If you're writing for a specific performer then you will need to use their physical traits and mannerisms, but otherwise it's up to you.

You'll be making certain choices for the character, regarding appearance, speech, and behaviour. In all of them it's important to keep them consistent throughout the piece. You can of course deliberately take them out of the bounds you've created for them, but there has to be a reason. If an immaculately dressed character is suddenly scruffy or a softly spoken one starts shouting, this will signal to the audience that something major has happened.

## Simple comedy situations

Stock situations are extremely useful to the comedy writer. At the most basic level, a cartoonist only has to draw a palm tree and a little hump and we know straightaway it's a 'stranded on a desert island' joke. Examples of other stock situations are:

▶ Angels on a cloud
▶ In the doctor's waiting room
▶ Couple sitting on the sofa
▶ In a restaurant
▶ In a shop
▶ In a pub
▶ In the office.

As well as in cartoons, this type of situation occurs over and over again in sketches, quickies and sitcoms. Using them takes away the need for an elaborate set-up and puts the audience straight into the action.

Situations also need comedy potential. On the whole that means choose places where people interact and where there is the potential for conflict. That's why all forms of customer services are so fruitful – shops, reception areas, car salerooms and so on.

Exercise

**Make a list of ten situations with comedy potential.**

# Things to remember

▶ Every character has a unique voice.

▶ Comedy often uses simple stereotypes.

▶ Conflict can be inner, with other people or with society.

▶ There are recurring character types in comedy.

▶ Find characters by observation.

▶ Comedy characters can range from realistic to grotesquely exaggerated.

▶ There are standard comedy situations.

▶ Choose situations where people have to interact with each other.

# 8

......................................................................................

# Sketches and quickies

In this chapter you will learn:
- *about quickies*
- *about sketches*
- *about sketch options*.

A sketch is like a long joke, and usually runs for between two and eight minutes, whereas a quickie is more like a one liner with just a set-up and a punchline. There is no room in either for unnecessary words or lines and so they make excellent writing practice.

Both require simple situations that an audience can understand instantly and a small number of characters. There's no time to develop characters so you need a very clear understanding of each one and you need to convey that to the audience. Characters for quickies are very simply drawn. For sketches, each character will need a single dominant characteristic and some sort of conflict that will drive the sketch forward.

......................................................................................

**Comedy insight – KEV F SUTHERLAND**

*The most common mistake that new comedy writers make is writing stuff that can't be performed. Whether you're writing sketches, stand-up, plays, TV, sitcom, you're writing material to be performed and you are always going to need to keep the audience's attention. Reading your work out loud, or better getting someone else to read it, can help.*

Kev F Sutherland is a comedian and comic artist (*Beano, Marvel, Viz*, etc.)

......................................................................................

_____

## Quickies

Quickies are often just a joke acted out, and usually end with a blackout (on stage) or a camera cut or pullback (on TV).

The pullback reveals a visual punchline. Because they are so quick they must be simple and cheap to do – no fancy special effects. There are endless variations to be had from two people talking:

> Boy: *They said in Assembly taking E destroys your memory like.*
>
> Girl: *What destroys your memory?*
>
> Boy: *I dunno, who told you that?*
>
> Girl: *Told me what?*

You can also write linked quickies, where a whole series of characters come into the same situation, with a bigger laugh for each one. If they are performed consecutively, then it's more like a sketch than a series of quickies.

## Writing quickies

To write a quickie, start with an easily recognized situation and introduce one or two characters.

Write a quickie for each of the situations from the list you created for the previous chapter. Use characters from your character list.

Use the same techniques to generate quickies as you used for short jokes, but remember to think visually. Sometimes you don't need dialogue at all:

> *Scene: supermarket car park*
>
> *We see an elderly lady struggling with a full trolley – she spots a handsome young customer care assistant and waves him over. He pushes her trolley to the car. She opens the car, pushes him in and drives off, leaving the trolley.*

Write a quickie with no dialogue for each of the situations on your list. Use characters from your character list.

Remember that even if you're writing for radio, you'll still need to create pictures for the listeners. In fact the visual side of radio comedy is worth exploiting to the full, because you can be as surreal and illogical as you like:

> *Police who found 66 pounds of cocaine in the nose cone of a jumbo jet became suspicious after it refused to land and kept circling the airport making whooping noises.*

> *A blind man has paddled a canoe round Britain in five months. He would've been quicker, but the dog kept chasing Channel Ferries.*

Once you have a good set-up for a quickie, see if you can get more than one joke out of it by doing a series. For instance an office setting is simple to create and has endless possibilities:

**Scene: man and woman both working at their desks.**

*Man:*   *Oi! Sellotape!*

**Woman throws it over to him**

*Woman:*   *I want that back. I know what you're like. Take the blouse off my back given half a chance you would.*

*Man:*   *Oh stop your moaning.*

*Woman:*   *Me! What about you…* (phone rings, she answers it) *Hello – Society of Friends.*

Once the principle is established, the joke can be reworked for any number of settings. For instance: people playing = Child Psychiatry; people struggling to add up coffee money = Institute of Accountants; people asleep = Energy Saving Trust; people getting lost on the way to their desks = Institute of Navigation. Try to raise the comedy stakes a little for each one, and save a good one for last:

*Scene:*   **Man and woman both working at their desks.**

*Man:*   *So I came off the motorway and got onto the old A38, completely empty, not a car in sight, and I made up all the time I'd lost, even stopped at a little country pub for lunch, lovely it was, just like a place I went to on holiday in Devon a couple of years ago, no tell a lie, it was the North York Moors, wonderful inglenook fireplace, middle of nowhere, right off the beaten track, I was staying a few miles away in a little B and B, recommended to me by my mother's cousin, don't know*

*if I mentioned her, she's got a wooden leg, married a
chap from Derby, Edwina Currie used to be her M. P.,
of course she's from Liverpool originally, I went to
Liverpool once...*

(phone rings, woman answers it)

**Woman:** *Hello – Ramblers Association.*

Exercise

EXERCISE

See how many variations you can find on one quickie.

_____

## Sketches

Traditionally sketches are based on one idea and tell the story of a
single incident. As the sketch unfolds there are several laughs building
to the punchline. The set-up for a sketch is known as the premise
and it needs to be established very quickly indeed. Once the action
has started there should be a moment when the audience knows that
things are going to go wrong.

The premise is very important, the whole sketch hangs from it, so it
must be strong enough to drive the action but equally not too big –
don't choose something that needs a half-hour sitcom or a full-length
novel to do it justice.

On a practical note, remember that sketches have a limited budget.
A simple set is all you can expect on stage, and for TV don't write in
special effects, location filming, night filming or anything else that
will be expensive.

........................................................................................

**Comedy insight – SUE LIMB**

*My favourite comedy comes from characters passionately engaged
in serious stuff and not realizing that they're being funny.*

Sue Limb is a comedy writer

(Dulcie Domum, *Up the Garden Path, The Wordsmiths at Gorsemere*)

........................................................................................

_____

## Writing sketches

There are two basic ways of writing sketches. Sometimes you have an
idea for a complete sketch. All you have to do is write it out and then

edit and polish it – which is still quite a lot of work. More often than not however you'll have only the vaguest idea or even no idea at all, in which case you'll have to start from scratch.

The techniques that you learned for joke writing will stand you in good stead here.

### BASIC SITUATION AND CHARACTERS

Let's look at the detail of writing a sketch. It's going to be about funerals. The easily recognized funeral situation is mourners standing round the open grave, but that requires location filming and in any case most people are cremated these days. We could set it in the church or crematorium but those are quite complicated sets. For a one-off sketch, the actual funeral parlour is the easiest to set up, and this would also work in a theatre.

Exercise

Choose a situation for your sketch.

As for characters, obviously there are the bereaved and the undertakers. We could consider new staff in the undertakers, comically inappropriate, or a customer who is under some sort of misapprehension and isn't actually bereaved at all. To keep it simple, I'll choose an undertaker and a customer who is there to deal with some aspect of the funeral process.

Exercise

Choose two characters from the lists you've already made.

### GENERATING IDEAS

Once you have the situation and characters, make lists of everything you can think of relating to them, exactly as you did for joke writing. The comedy must come from either the characters or the situation, and the lists will stop you being distracted as you write.

*Funeral, undertaker, hearse, black, flowers, different funeral packages, corpse, embalming, urn, ashes, coffins, reincarnation, heaven and hell, headstone, memorial and so on.*

Make lists relating to the situation and characters you've chosen.

Next take each word on your list and look for connections, opposites, alternative uses, visual jokes, wordplays and clichés. For instance:

> *Funeral – ceremony, mourners, procession, burial, cremation, wedding, christening, gone to a better place, funeral contains the syllable 'fun', arguing over the will.*

Exercise

Look for connections, opposites, alternative uses, visual jokes, wordplays and clichés.

Spend a little time thinking about the jokes that these generate – it helps get you right inside the topic, and some of them will end up in the sketch. There are plenty of funeral jokes:

> *One Saturday afternoon a funeral procession passes the football ground. A fan takes his hat off and bows his head. His friend says 'That's a really nice gesture.' 'It's the least I can do,' says the bloke 'She was a good wife to me for over 40 years.'*

> *Headstone: Here lies an Atheist, all dressed up and nowhere to go.*

> *A passenger in a taxi tapped the driver on the shoulder to ask him a question. The driver screamed, lost control of the cab, nearly hit a bus, drove up the curb, and stopped just inches from a large plate glass window. The driver said 'I'm sorry, you scared the daylights out of me. Today is my first day driving a cab... I've been driving a hearse for the last 25 years.'*

Exercise

Look for the jokes.

### ASKING THE RIGHT QUESTIONS

Once you've warmed up your comedy muscles with jokes around the topic, move on to the sketch. The most important questions to ask are 'What can go wrong?' and 'What if'. Ask those questions about everything on your lists, then look through for funny items that hang nicely together.

The answer to the question 'What can go wrong at a funeral?' is 'almost anything', although by confining ourselves to the funeral parlour we can't, for instance, use the old joke of a drunk falling into the grave – unless of course it's described after the event. In any case, because funerals are important and emotional affairs, people generally want them to run smoothly. So anything going wrong produces a heightened response. Another list is called for:

> *Someone could have fallen in the grave, the undertaker could be drunk, the undertaker could be working his notice and be in the mood for trouble, the family could fall out over what they want, the wife and the mistress could both turn up at the funeral parlour, the coffin could fall to bits.*

Exercise

Ask 'What can go wrong?'

Now for the What ifs. Don't be tempted to overlap with the first question (e.g. What if the undertaker was drunk?) – this is your chance to explore connections and reach for the bizarre:

> *What if the undertaker had a second job as a stripagram? What if the funeral parlour was being redecorated? What if business was quiet and they were using the hearse to sell ice-cream? What if the customer was looking for a buy-one-get-one-free deal? What if the customer was a gangster looking for a bulk discount? What if the undertaker really wanted to be a lumberjack?*

Exercise

Ask 'What if?'

By now something should be leaping out at you – if it isn't, then keep going with more lists, jokes and questions. But in this case, I keep being drawn back to one thing – the first syllable of funeral is 'fun'. This prompts more list making for ways of connecting funerals to fun:

*Tap dancing on the coffin, sawing the coffin in half, party in the church, the dead parrot sketch, pall-bearers dressed as clowns, Chapel of Jest.*

Exercise

Decide what's leaping out at you and develop it.

### FINE-TUNING THE CHARACTERS

It's time to think more about the characters. If you're writing for specific performers, you'll know about their strengths and weaknesses and that will have a bearing on the characters you create for them. If the situation is inherently funny, have a least one character who is unaware of this. If the situation is straightforward, then have at least one character who is funny. In the case of the funeral sketch, it looks as if the comedy is going to arise out of the connection between funerals and fun, so the characters need to be fairly straightforward.

There's always a danger of overloading a sketch. So how about an undertaker who appears stereotypically solemn and a little pompous, while at the same time treating fun funerals as completely normal, and a customer who is outraged at the idea but who is struggling to maintain her dignity at a difficult time.

Is she the bereaved person? Has she arranged the funeral, or has she come in afterwards to pay the bill, or maybe to pick up the ashes? The situation before a funeral is far tenser, which would probably produce a lot of comic possibilities, but we'd be in danger of poking fun at bereaved people's suffering. That would make for some fairly black comedy. Let's set the sketch after the funeral, when someone comes along to pay the bill.

Exercise

Make decisions about your characters.

The next task is to choose from your various lists. Look for at least three good jokes, and work out an order that will save the best till last.

Exercise

Choose items from your lists that will hang together to make your sketch.

### PLOTTING

Does a sketch need a plot? Just a little one. The simplest plot consists of three elements. First there is the set-up or basic situation, then the trigger that sets events in motion and finally the pay-off that resolves things. In other words, it's a lot like joke writing, and now you'll be glad you practised the skills.

So once you've chosen the best jokes, and looked at an order for them, consider what story they are going to tell. The key is to keep it very simple – a sketch can't bear the weight of a complicated storyline.

For the funeral sketch we'll have a simple linear plot – a woman comes in to pay her bill and it all unfolds from there.

Exercise

**Create a simple plot for your sketch.**

### WRITING A DRAFT

We already have the set-up of someone turning up to pay the bill for a funeral.

The opening needs to swiftly set the scene:

> *A WOMAN ENTERS A FUNERAL PARLOUR.*
>
> *Undertaker:   May one be of assistance?*
>
> *Woman:   Um... yes... it's a bit awkward.*
>
> *Undertaker:   Modom has come to make arrangements for the dear departed? Rest assured, we are professionals.*
>
> *Woman:   No, no, it's not that...*
>
> *Undertaker:   Modom is aware that this is a funeral parlour?*
>
> *Woman:   (Angry) Is it? Are you sure? (Makes an effort at self-control. Produces a piece of paper.) Actually it's about this bill of yours...*

This is the moment when the audience knows something is wrong – the trigger or Uh-oh moment.

Exercise

**Write the opening, with the set-up and the Uh-oh moment.**

*The Undertaker is unperturbed:*

**Undertaker:** (taking the bill from her) *Ah yes. Funeral of Mr Johnson. I take it Modom is here on behalf of Mrs Johnson?*

**Woman:** *Yes. She's my aunt. She couldn't come. She's a bit upset you see.*

**Undertaker:** *Quite understandable. The grieving widow.*

**Woman:** *Not about that. Well naturally she is upset about that, we all are, and then there was the funeral, that was quite distressing, and then when the bill came it was the last straw. It is a lot of money.*

**Undertaker:** *Mrs Johnson requested our top of the range funeral. The Jeeves.*

And this is the moment when the audience starts to get a clue about what is going on. Jeeves is a very odd name for a funeral package, and we can reasonably expect the majority of people to make the connection with Jeeves and Wooster.

**Woman:** *Yes. You see, she is rather elderly. I'm not sure that she entirely understood the, er, the implications.*

**Undertaker:** *And then there is the extra charge for the services of the embalmer. Did you view the deceased in our Chapel of Jest?*

Now the audience should be in no doubt, assuming the performer has clear diction and puts enough weight on the word 'jest'.

*Exercise*

Finish the opening section of your sketch, to the point where the set-up is fully established.

Time to get into the meat of the sketch and slot in the various jokes:

**Woman:** *Yes. Quite a shock.*

**Undertaker:** *So very lifelike. One almost expects the deceased to leap out of the coffin…*

**Woman:** *…and say 'Mr Grimsdale!'*

**Undertaker:** *Ah yes, you had the Norman Wisdom. Very impressive.*

Woman: *Considering my uncle was 6'3" and 16 stone.*

Undertaker: *A triumph of the embalmer's art. Only possible when expense is no object.*

Woman: *It certainly wasn't cheap. And did we really need two priests for the service?*

Undertaker: *That is standard with the Jeeves.* (Woman looks puzzled.) *For the dead parrot sketch at the altar?* (Does a bad imitation of John Cleese) *'This is an ex-parrot'?*

Woman: (not amused). *Yes. I was there. I think we'd have preferred it without the, er, frills.*

Undertaker: *Is Modom referring to our basic funeral, the Coco? It lacks the richness of the Jeeves, but the priest does wear a red nose and a revolving bow tie instead of his dog collar. A little obvious perhaps, but most effective for a certain class of person.*

Woman: *It's just that it's not what we were expecting.*

Undertaker: *No? Surely Mrs. Johnson understood the nature of our service to the bereaved?* (He reveals a poster on the wall which reads 'we put the FUN back in FUNERAL')

Woman: *My aunt just wanted to do the best for her husband.*

Undertaker: *Quite so Modom. The Jeeves was clearly the most suitable. Everything of the best. Finest mahogany coffin, very solid...*

Woman: *...that's true. The poor chap had quite a struggle to saw it in half.* (She takes out her credit cards) *Look, I just want to pay the bill and forget about the whole thing. How much altogether?*

Undertaker: *That all depends on Modom's final decision. Regarding the ashes?* (He produces three identical urns from beneath the counter.)

Woman: *Which one is it?*

Undertaker: *That one* (He takes the lid off, shows her the ashes, replaces the lid.) *Keep your eye on it.* (He swaps them round rapidly.) *Choose one.*

*Woman:*   *Er... that one?*

*Undertaker:*   *Sure?*

*Woman:*   *Yes. No. Oh, that one.* (She opens an urn. A boxing glove on a spring pops out.)

*Undertaker:*   *Modom wasn't paying attention was Modom? It's this one of course.* (He gives her the correct urn). *We can arrange disposal if required.*

Exercise

Write the main body of your sketch.

### ENDING A SKETCH

The biggest problem for most sketch writers is the pay-off and ending. In fact a lot of classic sketches don't end especially well. Even Monty Python's wonderful Lumberjack sketch ends fairly weakly with the girlfriend running off in tears. The psychopathic barber who wants to be a lumberjack was a great (and rather complicated) premise, but the ending was problematic.

If you watch a few classic sketches (The Two Ronnies 'Fork Handles', Victoria Wood 'Two Soups' and so on) you'll see that there are big laughs all the way through and quite often a smaller laugh at the end, but the ending is almost always a surprise – just enough to create the last laugh and round the sketch off. The key to the surprise is that it is both logical and unpredictable – yes that's right, just like joke writing.

At the end of 'Two soups' the surprise is that the elderly waitress, who has seemed so subservient and willing to oblige, swears when she doesn't get a tip. And yet it is logical too, because she must have had so many dissatisfied customers who didn't tip her that she's bound to have grown grumpy about it.

Another option for the ending is to come full circle and return to the beginning of the sketch.

A series of sketches that feature the same characters can all have the same ending. For instance a lot of Little Britain's Vicky Pollard sketches end with the line 'don't go giving me evils' – her ultimate riposte to whichever authority figure is trying to sort her out.

It's time to head for the end of the 'Funeral Fun' sketch:

**Woman:** (clutching the urn protectively) *I don't want my uncle turned into sneezing powder!*

**Undertaker:** *Ah, very funny Modom. I'm afraid the ashes of deceased persons would never meet the required standard for sneezing powder. We merely place the ashes in the Garden of Remembrance.*

**Woman:** *No tricks? No jokes?*

**Undertaker:** *Indeed no. Unless you count... but it is a very small one.*

**Woman:** *A very small what?*

**Undertaker:** *A very small rollercoaster. Like the rest of the rides. Of course we do have rather a large Haunted House.*

**Woman:** *More a Funfair of Remembrance really. I don't think my uncle would have wanted that.*

**Undertaker:** *Was the deceased a little lacking in humour perhaps?*

**Woman:** *You can say that again. He was a traffic warden. Very zealous. Even gave me a ticket once!*

**Undertaker:** *Dear dear.*

**Woman:** *I was picking my aunt up from the doctor's. His wife! She was on crutches at the time. And I was only giving her a lift because he was too mean to pay for a taxi.*

They both stare at the urn.

**Woman:** *Bastard.*

**Undertaker:** *Ex-bastard.*

**Woman:** *He didn't like Norman Wisdom you know. Well he didn't like any of them. Couldn't take a joke. He would have hated that funeral. Hated it.* (She smiles)

**Undertaker:** *Modom is feeling better?*

**Woman:** *Oh yes. Yes indeed.*

She laughs. The undertaker looks smug.

Exercise

Write the end of your sketch.

If you're submitting work to an existing sketch show, stick with what you know the performers can do. Only established writers get to push the boundaries.

# Editing

Once you've drafted the sketch it's time to edit and polish. And guess what, the skills you've already practised editing jokes will be useful with sketches. You still need to be economical with words, be specific, keep the best till last and so on. Oh, and don't throw anything away – add the rejects to your Spare Jokes folder.

Look at every speech and see if you can do without it. I think 'Funeral Fun' can manage without this exchange:

> **Woman:** ...*She couldn't come. She's a bit upset you see.*
>
> **Undertaker:** *Quite understandable. The grieving widow.*
>
> **Woman:** *Not about that. Well naturally she is upset about that, we all are, and then there was the funeral, that was quite distressing, and then when the bill came it was the last straw.*

Taking this out means that we get into the main part of the sketch much more quickly.

Next go through each speech and check that it is economical with words while still being in character. For instance 'Funeral Fun' can lose this 'A little obvious perhaps but most effective for a certain class of person.' It does add to the character of the Undertaker, but it isn't essential. Don't leave lines in that are funny but irrelevant, it's tough but you have to take them out.

Go through the sketch and mark where you think the laughs will be. Are there any that are too close together? Or any long gaps without a laugh? Check that nothing crucial is said or done immediately after a laugh.

Finally have a good look at the ending. Does it fit the premise? If not, and it goes off at a surreal tangent, are you sure the audience will be able to follow? As with most sketch drafts the ending of 'Funeral Fun' does seem a little weak. The focus is on the uncle. His personality hasn't been described earlier in the sketch, and the fact that he was a thoroughly unpleasant man only appears at the end, which means that the sketch has gone off at a tangent. The question is, is that funny enough for the ending? How about ending the sketch when the boxing glove pops out of the urn? This keeps to the premise of the sketch, which is about mixing comedy with funerals. On the other hand it means losing a speech that potentially has quite a lot of laughs in it:

> **Woman:** *I was picking my aunt up from the doctor's.* (laugh)
> *His wife!* (laugh) *She was on crutches at the time.*
> (laugh) *And I was only giving her a lift because he*
> *was too mean to pay for a taxi.* (laugh)

So maybe the place to end the sketch is on the line 'Ex-bastard', which has a nice echo of 'ex-parrot'. It moves away from the premise, but does mean that it ends on a twist. So which ending to go for? I'm not sure – what do you think?

*Exercise*

Edit your sketch, mark the laughs, and fine tune the ending.

---

## Sketch options

There are several tried and tested formats for sketches.

### *TRAVELLING IN TIME*

Either project into the future, or go backwards into history. Always pick something that the audience is going to recognize instantly – Queen Victoria talking to Disraeli rather than Tennyson talking to his wife (unless of course there has recently been a successful costume drama about Tennyson, putting him back in the public eye).

You can also use anachronisms, where a character brings 21st century attitudes into the past. This is the basis for Armstrong and Miller's Second World War airmen who use current street jargon.

*Exercise*

Devise a situation and characters for a time travel sketch.

### *SEND-UP OR PARODY*

Again it has to be something instantly recognizable, so choose something currently successful – a current movie or TV programme, a celebrity who is in the news and so on.

Devise a parody sketch.

### REVERSAL

This basically means having characters do the opposite of what the audience expects. Put a stereotypical character in an unfamiliar situation – for instance, a doctor at home, talking to his wife as if she were a patient.

Write a reversal sketch using a situation and characters from your earlier lists.

---

## Things to remember

▶ Keep the set-up simple.

▶ Consider writing a series with the same set-up.

▶ Remember there are budget and technical constraints.

▶ The comedy must arise from the characters and their situation.

▶ Use lists to generate ideas around a topic.

▶ Warm up by writing jokes on the topic.

▶ Ask yourself 'What can go wrong' and 'What if'.

▶ Don't overload a sketch with too much character and story.

▶ Put extra effort into the ending.

▶ Edit for economy and focus.

# 9

## More complex characters

In this chapter you will learn:
- **to create more developed characters**
- **to understand the need for conflict and flaws**
- **to combine characters.**

*Exercise note: over the next few chapters you will create characters, a situation and a plot for a short piece. It can be a sitcom episode, a short story or a one-act play – your choice.*

So far we've looked at the simple characters needed for stand-up, quickies, sketches and cartoons. For longer formats such as sitcoms, novels, plays and movies, the characters need to be more complex but still very crisply conceived and fully developed. (Some longer comedies take characters onto a different level, which we'll look at in Chapter 12.)

In this type of comedy characters are more complex but are still fixed and the laughs come from what happens around them and their reactions to situations. Conflict is still the most important requirement, but now you need to create characters that are more fully rounded. Stock characters and stereotypes are no longer useful, except perhaps in bit parts – characters for the longer formats need to be highly individual.

Characters need to be flawed in some way, and the flaw will arise from their inner conflict. Many comedy characters have flaws that the rest of us understand only too well, which is why we feel a connection with them. We can see our own failings reflected back to us. At the same time, one of the reasons we laugh at their misfortune rather than commiserate is that we can see they only have themselves to blame. So Father Ted is a lazy priest who can't be trusted with money and Dave Lister (*Red Dwarf*) is a slob who never does anything properly.

Most successful comedy characters are basically likeable despite their failings – Bertie Wooster, Del Boy (*Only Fools and Horses*), Geraldine (*The Vicar of Dibley*) and so on. And there are other characters that we like because they get away with the things that we would love to do ourselves – Bernard Black in *Black Books* is rude to customers and shuts his shop when he feels like it but is still a likeable character.

However there is a separate category of deeply unlikeable and unredeemed characters who are still comedically successful. We don't feel a connection with characters like Alan Partridge and David Brent (*The Office*), but the chances are we know someone like them. In real life they can be almost impossible to deal with – thick-skinned, self-centred, deluded – so it is amusing and satisfying to see how their fictional counterparts dig themselves ever deeper into a bottomless pit.

Finally there are a small number of characters who are practically psychopathic, such as Jill Tyrell in *Nighty Night*. Inevitably the comedy is very dark, with as much pain as laughter, while we watch them ruin the lives of the innocent people around them and give thanks that we've never been the victim of someone like that.

**Comedy insight – RAY COONEY**
*If I had to give just one piece of comedy writing advice it would be: make it real.*

Ray Cooney is a playwright

# Creating characters

The simplest way to achieve rounded individual characters is to write a biography for each one so that you get to know them in depth. Most of this knowledge won't find its way into the finished work, but it will inform and underpin your writing.

Give each character a dominant trait or quirk and make them larger than life. The degree to which you do this will be part of what sets the tone for the comedy.

Here are some examples of short biographies, although the longer you make them the better you'll get to know your characters.

Adam 35 – *sees himself as a high flying executive but actually he has a merchandizing business putting company logos on T-shirts, mugs and biros. He still lives with his mum.*

Alex 40 – *only drives the best cars, wears the best suits and visits the most exclusive gyms. He works in finance so he doesn't get up in the morning for less than 10K and he believes money is there for spending.*

Colin 55 – *a middle-aged chauvinist with a beer gut and a strong conviction that women can't resist him. He considers himself the dominant male of any group. As far as he's concerned women don't count – he doesn't know that the one thing they all agree on is that Colin is disgusting.*

Danyella 16 – *is at that awkward age, it started when she was born and shows no sign of fading 16 years on. Her deepest relationship is with her mobile phone and she hates everyone older than 18.*

Laura 47 – *runs the House of Relaxation, a centre for massage, reflexology, aromatherapy, etc. She talks about auras and spirit healing but only half believes it all.*

Maisie 53 – *a middle-aged overweight party girl and born survivor. Sleeps all day and goes clubbing at night. Her only worry in life is wondering where she left her knickers.*

Norman 26 going on 50 – *super-geeky with a passion for counting things. He's never had a friend. In any group he wants to show off his knowledge but is always distracted by the need to check that everyone has a working biro.*

Stephanie 28 – *doesn't mind being a fat girl, because it means she can give people even better hugs, like a sort of primitive earth mother but with more sensitivity due to her reading of self-help books. She knows that anger is just love turned inside out so the more people shout at her the more she hugs them.*

Stuart 30 – *a naïve and insecure New Age type who lives off lentils and makes every sentence sound like a question.*

Wendy 25 – *a cynical young woman with a jaundiced view of the world. She has a computer science degree but finds it hard to get a job because of her chippy attitude.*

Write short biographies for ten comedy characters.

**Author insight**

If I'm working with several characters I keep a file on each one, adding to it as I write – to make sure I don't contradict myself.

### BACKGROUND AND BACK-STORY

You need to understand where the character comes from and how they reached the point they're at when the story starts. Are they, for instance, upwardly mobile or are they still in the house they were born in? Did they have a happy or unhappy childhood or did they do well or badly at school? Wherever they are, how did they get there, and why – there's a big difference between someone who is driven and someone who sits back and let's things happen.

Adam – *ordinary family background, not very successful at school, although he did learn to talk his way out of trouble, usually by telling lies based on his inner fantasies.*

Alex – *public school educated but not academic. The men in his family are either solicitors or doctors, so he constantly needs to prove that finance is just as important and difficult.*

Colin – *married his childhood sweetheart who divorced him when she discovered feminism, leaving him with a massive chip, possibly on his shoulder, possibly elsewhere.*

Danyella – *lives with her mum, her mum's boyfriend and several small children who are variously related to her and each other. Spends a lot of time round her Nan's.*

Laura – *like many twins she's determined to be different from her twin. Since Angela is married to a high-flying executive type with the lifestyle to match, Laura has gone the other way. Her gap year lasted a decade as she pursued an interest in alternative lifestyles. She doesn't have much money as a result, and she is secretly jealous of her sister's big house, smart cars and fancy holidays.*

Maisie – *used to work in a sweetie factory before it closed, famously the only employee who never got tired of sampling the product. Has definitely been married, and has children, but is vague about the details.*

Norman – *brought up by his doting mother after his dad left home following a row about the correct way to serve smoked salmon. She taught him it was never possible to be too tidy.*

Stephanie – *the oldest of a large family, she likes to be the mother-figure as it's all she knows.*

Stuart – *both his parents were hippies in the 60s, lived in a commune and when that broke down never really adjusted to the real world, where they are both teachers.*

Wendy – *an only child. Her middle-class aspirational mother was very competitive in all Wendy's activities, apart from social skills.*

Exercise

Create backgrounds for your characters.

### MOTIVATION, DOMINANT DESIRE AND FLAWS

We all have things that we think we ought to be doing ('I really ought to lose ten pounds', 'I really ought to clean the car') but unless those things somehow connect with our deep motivation in life we probably won't get round to doing them. So if your character's key motivation is vanity, then they will probably lose the weight while driving round in a filthy car, whereas the reverse might be true of someone whose key motivation was to maintain their social standing.

Successful comedy characters need an obvious and simple key motivation that audiences can identify with. Of course comedy is full of odd, quirky and eccentric characters, but their motivation is usually on the surface for everyone to see. *The Vicar of Dibley* is packed to the church rafters with eccentrics but every one is clearly drawn with easily understood motivation: David Horton needs to be in charge, over-sexed Owen Newitt ignores the conventions of polite society, Leticia Cropley loves to cook but has no sense of taste, and so on.

However, all of us have deeper drives that are not so obvious, even to ourselves, and the same is true of comedy characters. Why is the vain character vain? Is it because he or she was a plain child, and constantly teased about their appearance? Or is it the opposite, that they were good-looking when young and are determined to hang on to the kudos it brings them?

When you're creating characters they will be much more real if you work out what their deep motivation is, but you don't have to reveal this to the audience, and the character doesn't have to be aware of it. In *The Vicar of Dibley* we do get insight into downtrodden Hugo Horton because we meet his father but the other characters mainly keep their secrets. In fact keeping that knowledge to yourself can make a character more realistic, since very few of us are aware of our deep motivation (unless, of course, we've had years of expensive therapy). Some writers think keeping the core secret about characters is the key to success.

### Author insight

The first draft of my novel *Going Through the Motions* had a lot about the main character's childhood (her father was a ladies' hairdresser, her mother drove a London bus) but in the second draft I took it all out – it was enough for me to know how her character was formed.

A character's dominant desire arises out of their motivation and their reaction to their life situation. David Horton needs to be in charge of the Parish Council, but he could just as well be an office manager or an Army officer – the motivation and desire to run things would be the same.

Some of the explanation of motivation and dominant desire will come from a character's background and back-story, but don't forget that some things are inexplicable – some people are just born that way, and everybody is flawed in some way.

> Adam *wants other people to be impressed by his material success but hasn't got the talent to be successful. Lazy.*

> Alex *is only interested in money and has no spiritual depth. Greedy.*

Colin *still lives by outdated macho beliefs and has no self-insight. Bullying.*

Danyella *lives in the moment with no thought for tomorrow. Self-centred.*

Laura *is drawn to the world of alternative therapies because she likes the hippy image but doesn't really believe in any of it. Manipulative.*

Maisie *just wants to have a good time and never got round to growing up. Thoughtless.*

Norman *wants to organize the world and has no empathy with other people. Over-intense.*

Stephanie *is terrified of looking inside herself, so focuses on caring for other people. Greedy.*

Stuart *is unable to engage with harsh reality. Impractical.*

Wendy *wants to impress people with her cleverness. Rude.*

Exercise

Work out the motivation, dominant desires and flaws of your characters.

### THE UNSEEN CHARACTER

The unseen character can be a useful source of comedy, because they can be far more extreme than a character that we meet. Of course they can only ever be a minor character but they add another layer of comedy. You can see the different effects in *The Good Life*, where we never meet the two characters who plague Margo Ledbetter, Miss Mountshaft of the Music Society and Mrs Dooms-Paterson of the Pony Club. We do however meet Sir, Tom's ex-boss and Jerry's current boss, in some episodes. Sir is set up as a megalomaniac and heartless boss, but inevitably he seems a little too human when we meet him. The two unseen characters are far more extreme.

You should develop the character fully, and take particular care to understand the dominant desire that causes them to behave as they do, and the nature of the relationship with the seen character.

### SELECTING CHARACTERS

Looking down your lists, which characters are you drawn to? We all have our own preferences, and as writers we'll create and work with characters that speak to us in some way.

> *I wouldn't want to write about Alex, but I could do something with Adam. Equally I wouldn't pick Stephanie because I don't see anything funny in weight issues, but I can see lots of comedy potential in two-faced Laura. Another writer might be able to make something out of Alex and Stephanie.*

Exercise

Assess your characters for comedy potential and decide which ones appeal to you as a writer.

### SUBTEXT AND AGENDAS

There is always more to a character than meets the eye. You may be talking to someone perfectly cheerfully but thinking about something else the whole time – how boring they are, what you fancy for your dinner, whether the gas bill is due yet and so on. For storytelling purposes these things need to be conveyed to the audience.

The broad spectrum of hidden meanings is known as subtext. Agendas are rather more specific. Someone has an agenda when they go into a situation knowing what they want to get out of it. We all do it, and it has great comedy potential. For instance, a man wants to get to a football match but his partner insists that he help her choose new cushions. As long as his love of football has been set up in advance, there are a lot of laughs to be gained from the way he will want to buy the first cushions they see, suitably hideous of course, and will pay through the nose for them. Then when his partner tells him to take them home with him, naturally he'll take them to the football match instead, and they'll get damaged in some way, or he'll lose them and have to find others.

Subtext and agendas are not the same as internal conflict. A character's internal conflict doesn't change, whereas their subtext and agendas change according to the situation. However a character's dominant desire will usually be the driving force behind their agenda in any given situation.

### BODY LANGUAGE

Apparently we reveal more about our thoughts through body language than through what we say. For instance, someone scratching their neck is supposed to be doubting the truth of what they're hearing. A character like No Offence, the beauty advisor in *The Fast Show*, has obsequious body language while making offensive remarks, which adds to the comedy. In the same show the body language of Ted and Ralph is what tells us there is something going on under the surface of the master/servant relationship.

### VOICE

Consider how your character speaks – Received Pronunciation or strong regional accent? Which region? When you're thinking about this, remember that English audiences have ingrained presumptions about accents. Scots are canny, Londoners are fly, country people are slow and so on. When you're writing jokes, sketches and quickies you can make use of these stock qualities, but otherwise only use them if they absolutely meet your writing needs.

When you first start writing you'll find that you choose voices based on your own favourite fictional characters. Once you've corrected that habit you might tend to give all your characters your own voice. And once you've corrected that habit you can get down to giving characters their own, unique voice.

### VOCABULARY

In the first draft of a piece you'll just be concerned to get the words down so you can reach the end of the draft, but part of the polishing process is to make sure each character has an appropriate vocabulary, and uses it consistently. Decide if they use slang or jargon, and if they do, decide if they are up to date or a bit behind the times.

### SPEECH PATTERN

Think about a character's speech pattern – do they talk fast in quick sentences, or have a slow ponderous delivery?

I hear these voices for my characters – you may hear others.

> **Adam** *uses slang and jargon that are out of date.*
>
> **Alex** *public school accent, uses jargon to baffle listeners.*
>
> **Colin** *Essex accent, talks tough.*

86

Danyella *uses teenage street talk, when she does talk – mainly she texts.*

Laura *softly spoken, has all the hippy-dippy vocabulary at the tip of her tongue.*

Maisie *Leeds accent, calls a spade a \*\*\*\*ing spade.*

Norman *hesitates a lot, because he's trying to be precise.*

Stephanie *chatters incessantly, loud laugh.*

Stuart *treats every sentence like a question and is very politically correct.*

Wendy *sharp-tongued, cynical and sarcastic.*

Exercise

Think about voice, vocabulary and speech pattern for your characters.

### NAMES

Naming a character is part of bringing it to life and can also tell the audience a lot about a character. Think about the probable differences between say, a Tarquin and a Derek. If you choose a funny name for your character, you'll be consigning it to the cartoonish, one-dimensional end of the spectrum – not necessarily a bad thing of course. Names can also give a clue as to the nature of the character – Fawlty, for instance, is clearly Faulty. When you're choosing names, think also about diminutives and pet names.

Exercise

Decide whether you're happy with the names you've given your characters.

........................................................................

**Comedy insight – SIMON BRETT**
> *Don't agonize over thinking of funny lines. If you've got the relationship between the characters right, the lines will come out funny.*

Simon Brett is a writer
........................................................................

# Characters combined

Once your characters are individually formed you have to
start putting them together. Contrasting characters give more
opportunities for comedy and a lot of comedy comes from conflict
between characters. Aim for a balance between eccentric characters
and relatively normal ones. For instance, in *Coupling* the characters
of Jane and Jeff are more eccentric than the other four characters,
which creates balance. Eccentric people are often unaware that
their behaviour is extreme, and so the reactions of the more normal
characters both underline the eccentricity and create laughs.

Looking down my list of characters, I like the look of Laura with
either Alex or Adam as a mismatched pair who would have plenty of
conflict, or maybe Norman and Maisie. Drippy Stuart with cold-
hearted Wendy is another possibility, although Wendy would also
struggle to get along with Danyella. Alex and Stephanie would have
endless conflict, as would Norman and Colin.

### Exercise

Decide which characters from your list would have comedy conflict.

#### BINDING TIES

Whatever type of situation you're putting them in, there is one big
question you'll need to answer. Why do they stand for it? If they
annoy each other so much, drive each other up the wall and round
the bend, why don't they just get out and away from each other?

The answer is something called binding ties, the unseen reasons why
characters stay together. Binding ties are the emotional connections that
keep us with people who drive us mad: we love our annoying teenage
children too much to kick them out of the house, we enjoy the income
produced by the job that frustrates us so much and we like the social
status of living in the exclusive road full of mind-bendingly dull people.

Some binding ties require deep psychological insight, although
you don't need to know the jargon. Words like co-dependency and
symbiosis are used to describe unhealthy relationships, but they
simply mean that people can be simultaneously unable to get on with
each other and yet need each other too.

For instance, the two characters in *Steptoe and Son* are always at each other's throats but still stay together. The audience is made aware that despite all his bluster and social ambitions, the son does actually need the father and would struggle without him. It's one of the staples of comedy writing and has to be very subtly done – too much and the whole thing turns schmaltzy, too little and the audience don't believe in the relationships.

This is another thing that you need to understand about your characters, but you don't have to reveal the whole picture.

Binding ties are particularly important in sitcoms, because characters stay together week after week, and this needs to be believable. As long as the ties are strong enough, the audience will accept the situation. Of course practical considerations are part of what keeps people together and those arise out of the situation they find themselves in – see Chapter 10 for more on this. The hardest ties to write well are the purely emotional ones – in *Keeping Up Appearances* it is hard to know why dreadful Hyacinth Bucket's husband and sisters put up with her, apart from the emotional ties.

For comedy purposes, characters who have binding ties with each other should want different things from life in order to create conflict. I'd pair my characters like this:

> **Adam/Laura** – *could be brother and sister or business contacts.*
>
> **Alex/Maisie** – *co workers. Maisie could be the cleaner in Alex's office.*
>
> **Colin /Norman** – *neighbours.*
>
> **Danyella /Stephanie** – *student and school counsellor.*
>
> **Stuart /Wendy** – *unlikely to be boyfriend/girlfriend, could be siblings or co-workers.*

Exercise

Work out binding ties for the characters on your list who have the most conflict.

Dialogue between characters is multifunctional. It conveys character, moves the plot forward and gives information. If you're writing for performance, dialogue will be your main means of communication with an audience, whereas prose writers have the luxury of being able to describe a character's inner workings.

Drafting out sample dialogue is the quickest way to get to know how your characters interact with each other. Early drafts don't have to be funny, they are part of the learning process, but you do need to get a feeling for where the comedy might come from.

> *Laura:*   (chanting) *Ohmmmm…*
>
> *Adam:*   *Good, great, lovely. Now I just had this idea…*
>
> *Laura:*   *…ohmmmm…*
>
> *Adam:*   *…just thought I'd run it up the flagpole and see how it fluttered…*
>
> *Laura:*   *…ohmmmm…*
>
> *Adam:*   *…you see what you need here is some marketing input. This room for instance…*
>
> *Laura:*   *There's nothing wrong with this room.*
>
> *Adam:*   *Wasted space. If you split it into two rooms you could rent one of them out and double your income.*
>
> *Laura:*   *I couldn't possibly. I need the space. I need to feel emptiness round me when I meditate.*
>
> *Adam:*   *Then there's the sound system. What's this we're listening to for instance?*
>
> *Laura:*   *Temple Bells. Very soothing.*
>
> *Adam:*   *Yes. But does it put people in the mood for spending? Will they go out of here primed and ready to choose from your display of organic relaxation products placed strategically next to the credit card facility?*
>
> *Laura:*   *We haven't got a display of relaxation products. Or a credit card facility.*
>
> *Adam:*   *No, but you will have, you will have.*

Write a sample dialogue for two of your characters who are in conflict. Don't struggle to make it funny at this stage, just write and see what happens.

Subtext can also be conveyed through speech, for instance via the Freudian slip. There are all sorts of explanations for this tendency to say one thing when you mean another, but for comedy purposes we assume the one that suggests it arises from what you're really thinking but would rather hide.

Another technique is to have a character express strong negative views about something that is clearly not true. A subtle variation of this is when a character appears to be talking about a third person but it becomes clear they are actually talking about themselves.

### SOMEONE TO CONFIDE IN

If you're writing for performance, you're likely to find that your main character needs a sidekick, someone to share things with and someone who helps them out. There will still be some conflict no doubt, but basically they will be on the same side. For performance this is one of the best ways of conveying the detail of a character's thoughts. Prose writers of course can dive straight in and tell their readers, but the sidekick is still useful – too much description of a character's inner thoughts can send a reader off to sleep.

I could arrange sidekicks like this:

> Adam/Wendy – *both lack social skills so have no other friends.*

> Alex/Norman – *Alex is a show-off and Norman would admire him.*

> Colin/Stephanie – *Stephanie is too soft-hearted to tell Colin to push off.*

> Danyella/Maisie – *share the same interests.*

> Laura/Stuart – *two of a kind but Stuart wouldn't see through Laura's hypocrisy.*

These all look reasonable apart from Colin and Stephanie, which isn't a natural pairing – Colin would want a mate to watch football

with, and Stephanie would be more likely to latch on to Norman. I'd
need to create new sidekicks for those two.

## Exercise

Rearrange your characters into pairs with less conflict and more chance
of being friends.

Although there is conflict in the relationship, at the same time there is
friendship, or something close to it. In the sitcom *Miranda*, Miranda
confides in her friend Stevie while at the same time she is often pretty
horrid to her. The fact that they work together provides a binding tie.

Again it's a good idea to draft out some dialogue so you can learn
how the characters interact.

| | |
|---|---|
| Stuart: | *The thing about people dying, Laura, it's just like, so so stressful?* |
| Laura: | *Yes. Yes it is. Let's breathe the stress away Stuart. Take in a breath, then let it out slowly. Slowly. Slooooowly.* |
| Stuart: | *It's no good, I can't do it.* |
| Laura: | *Stuart, just...* |
| Stuart: | *It's like, the appointment book? All these pages set aside for Margaret? What can I do with them Laura? What can I do?* |
| Laura: | *Well, er, take them out and...* |
| Stuart: | *Yes! I will! I will take them out and I'll put them with Margaret's candle. That way we can still remember her, but I won't be haunted by her empty pages in the appointment book.* |
| Laura: | *Yes. Life is a mystery, don't you think?* |
| Stuart: | *Oh yes. Laura...* |
| Laura: | *And death. Death is a mystery too.* |
| Stuart: | *Yes. Laura, you know the appointment book is empty. I mean your side? Your side of the book is empty for today. And tomorrow.* |
| Laura: | *Margaret did say a tree didn't she?* |
| Stuart: | *And next week.* |

| Laura: | *Definitely coming back as a tree?* |
| Stuart: | *Yes. A silver birch. A lovely floppy one.* |
| Laura: | *It's just that, they are rather large.* |
| Stuart: | *We could plant her outside.* |
| Laura: | *Ah, she'd be lonely outside.* |
| Stuart: | *Oh no. She'd like to see the sun. And the moon.* |

Exercise

Write a short dialogue for two of your characters who are friends.

---

## Things to remember

▶ Give each character a flaw and conflict.

▶ Most comedy characters are likeable.

▶ Develop biographies for your characters.

▶ Understand their background.

▶ Understand their motivation and dominant desires.

▶ Choose characters that you're drawn to.

▶ Understand their inner workings.

▶ Body language and speech reveal character.

▶ Binding ties keep characters together.

▶ Everyone needs someone to talk to.

# 10

# More complex situations and plots

In this chapter you will learn:
- **about conflict and claustrophobia**
- **how to construct a plot**
- **about endings**.

As well as strong funny characters, longer forms of comedy need
a plot. This can be anything from a tightly crafted traditional farce
to the much looser requirements of a diary-format novel. In comedy
writing, plots are often circular, returning characters to the place
they started out from – this is especially true of sitcoms. Although
a sitcom plot needs to tell a story, the payoff, or resolution, will
bring everything back to the status quo ready for next week's
episode.

### DO PLOTS HAVE TO BE FUNNY?

Here's an example of a comedy plot:

> *A man's annoying behaviour drives his wife to the point of
> divorce. When she throws him out, he decides to try to kill
> himself, so his best friend takes him in. He gradually annoys his
> friend so much that he throws him out, but immediately regrets
> it in case it prompts another suicide attempt. After searching
> the city for his friend, he finally finds him staying with some
> neighbours. They make their peace with each other and their
> friendship is saved.*

Not a lot of laughs in that perhaps – except it's the plot of *The
Odd Couple*, one of the all time great comedy movies. So clearly

a comedy plot doesn't have to be amusing in itself. Here's another example:

> *Two musicians witness a gangland killing and go into hiding disguised as women. They join an all-female band. One of them is attracted to a beautiful fellow band member and in order to woo her he changes back into men's clothes and pretends to be a millionaire. He has constant costume changes and is often nearly caught out. The other one is pursued by a real millionaire who is fooled by his disguise and who proposes marriage. Everything is complicated by the fact that the gangsters are staying in the same hotel. In the end the musicians escape from the gangsters and both come clean about their disguises. Both the beautiful fellow band member and, surprisingly, the millionaire, are happy about this.*

Yes, that's right, it's *Some Like It Hot*, another all time great comedy movie, and one with a very funny plot.

So it's not necessary for your plot to be funny in itself but if it is you'll start ahead of the game in terms of getting laughs. You can also see that the plot of *Some Like It Hot* is far more complicated than *The Odd Couple*. Funny plots benefit from a lot of complications.

---

## Conflict and claustrophobia

For all forms of creative writing the situation you choose for your characters is absolutely critical. It needs to provide two elements: conflict and claustrophobia.

We've already looked at the three different types of conflict a character can experience (internal, interpersonal and societal) and clearly the situation you place them in can rack up the conflict.

Let's carry on working with the characters from Chapter 9.

> *The dialogue between Adam and Laura shows him trying to sell her his services which she doesn't really want. If they are related to each other, then she might find it difficult to turn him down but since her character is quite devious she'd probably find a way. On the other hand if they worked together there would be conflict because of their differing agendas, or they could be neighbours perhaps.*

**Create situations for your characters that will increase their conflict.**

Claustrophobia in this context simply means placing characters in situations they can't escape from, so that they have to find a way of rubbing along together. Binding ties are what make people stay together for emotional and psychological reasons. Claustrophobic situations force them together for practical reasons: changing jobs is not always an option, divorce is expensive, elderly parents need looking after and so on.

In *Steptoe and Son* the ties are both emotional (because they are father and son) and practical (because they run a business together). In *Porridge* the ties are entirely practical – the characters are in prison and have no choice about staying together.

*Red Dwarf* takes this to the ultimate extreme by marooning the characters in a spaceship. This definitely increases the conflict between the characters, but you can see the potential problem for a sitcom writer who needs to keep coming up with plots – the more isolated a group of characters are, the harder it is to think up new events that could happen to them. The writers of *Red Dwarf* needed to constantly engineer encounters with other spaceships, alien civilizations and so on.

Jane Austen was fully aware of the principle of claustrophobia when she wrote that for an author 'three or four families in a country village is the very thing to work on'. In the 18th century people were not as socially mobile as they are now, and so families tended to stay put in their home village. This gave her two levels of claustrophobia – within the family and within the small society of a village.

> *If Adam and Laura were working in the same office, there would have to be good reasons why neither of them could leave, which would increase the claustrophobia. They probably wouldn't choose to share premises, so it would need to be forced on them in some way.*

**Check your situations for claustrophobia – ask how easy it would be for the characters to walk away.**

................................................................
**Comedy insight – ANN GAWTHORPE**
*If I had to give just one piece of comedy writing advice it would be to know when to give the audience/reader prior information to create comedy – and when not to.*

Ann Gawthorpe is a writer
................................................................

## Creating a story

Conflicted characters and a claustrophobic situation aren't enough. You also need a story or plot. Sometimes it will be obvious from the characters and their situation what the story should be, but sometimes you'll have to start from scratch. Of course every basic story has already been told, but equally every old story can be reinterpreted and given a new twist. Here are some basic story ideas:

**The quest** This is one of the oldest story forms. A character sets out on a quest to find something and has adventures along the way. It doesn't have to be a physical journey – the quest can be for anything from a Golden Fleece to inner peace. Most stories in fact can be interpreted as quests.

**Love** Finding it, losing it and any associated complications. Recently Richard Curtis has been the king of love-based comedy with *Four Weddings and a Funeral*, *Notting Hill* and *Love Actually*.

**Hate** The trigger is something that causes the characters to fall out and the story is about how the argument escalates and is resolved. The Christmas TV drama *Christmas Lights* used the concept of two men falling out over who can create the most spectacular Christmas display, and was so successful it lead to two series and a second Christmas special.

**Accident** Stories based round accidents can give rise to a lot of physical comedy, for instance as a character struggles to go through their normal life with an arm or a leg in plaster.

**Sudden riches or poverty** Both situations produce great comedy. Sue Townsend sent the Queen to live on a council estate in *The Queen and I*, whereas *The Beverly Hillbillies* is about a poor family who strike it rich.

**An outsider** Any new person introduced into a stable set-up can cause comedy mayhem. An elderly parent moving in with their children and grandchildren, a new boss at work or someone retiring and being at home instead of at work.

**Special occasions** Weddings, Christmas, and other big life events can all make for good stories. A funeral can make a good plot trigger and divorce has proved to be fertile ground for sitcoms (*My Wife Next Door, Home To Roost, Teenage Kicks*) and movies (*Mrs Doubtfire, Liar Liar*).

**Something to hide** A protagonist with something to hide is a staple of traditional farce – in *Charley's Aunt* a man tries to pass himself off as the Aunt; he clearly has something to hide. It is also found in many other types of comedy.

**Misunderstandings** Another staple of farce that can be used in many ways. For instance, an early episode of *Men Behaving Badly* had Gary form a mistaken impression that his new flatmate Tony was gay.

**Incompetence** For many characters this would come under 'something to hide' but not always, for instance Frank Spencer in the classic sitcom *Some Mothers Do 'Ave 'Em* is quite openly useless.

**Fish out of water or role reversal** Any story that places a character in an unfamiliar environment has comedy potential.

**Moral or ethical issues** These may not seem the stuff of comedy but many plots hang on a moral dilemma, and the US series *My Name is Earl* is entirely about a small-time criminal who is trying to cancel out his bad past by doing good deeds.

### ROUGHING OUT A PLOT

Once you have a situation and an idea of what sort of plot you want to create it's time to start asking 'What if?' Let your answers be as far-fetched as possible. For each answer, ask 'What next?' Keep doing this until you find a sequence of events that will give you a plot. Choose the answers that walk the fine line between believable and ridiculous, and above all the ones that have the best comedy potential.

> *Adam and Laura work together in the same office. Adam is a marketing consultant, Laura does alternative therapies. The two businesses are not compatible. What if there was a mix-up in Reception and each of them saw the wrong client? How would a businessman feel about being asked to relax*

*and smell the roses? How would a New Age type feel about being given a marketing talk? Would they both storm out and refuse to pay? What if they both liked it and it changed their lives?*

## Exercise

Take your characters and situation of choice and rough out a plot for them for a one-act play or short story. (We'll look at sitcoms in the next chapter).

---

**Comedy insight – CHRIS RITCHIE**

*Be honest. Talk about what is real to you, what is believable. If an audience finds something funny as well as interesting, if they learn something, then the performance is going to be more memorable. Tell us something we don't know!*

Chris Ritchie created the innovative Comedy: Writing & Performance degree at
Southampton Solent University in 2006 and is the editor of *Comedy Studies*

---

### BACK-STORY, TRIGGER AND EXPOSITION

The back-story is everything that has happened to the characters up until the moment the story starts. Some of this will be revealed, some will remain hidden.

The trigger is the incident that sets the story in motion. Jane Austen understood that every story needs a trigger. In *Pride and Prejudice* for instance the trigger is the arrival of an eligible and wealthy young bachelor in the village.

In order to understand the significance of the trigger, the audience needs a certain amount of explanation about the characters and their situation – this is known as exposition. The challenge for the writer is to give all the information in a way that isn't too obvious or boring. *Pride and Prejudice* provides a masterclass in how to do this. In the first 300 words we learn that eligible Mr Bingley has moved to the area, that the Bennets have unmarried daughters, that Mrs Bennett wants to marry them off, and that Mr Bennett maintains a position of humorous detachment. We also as a result have a pretty good idea of the character of both Mr and Mrs Bennett and the way their marriage works, or doesn't work, and we've been both amused and engaged in the story.

Starting the story at the moment of the trigger ensures that the plot will engage the audience immediately, but it's not the only way to do it. The opening scene of the movie *Men in Black* is nine minutes long, and only reaches the trigger at the end of the scene, when Agent D decides to retire. The scene is a well crafted little story that sets the tone for the whole movie, with its mixture of comedy and drama. Of all the characters in the long opening sequence only Agent K is seen again, but a lot of information has been conveyed and the audience has been put into the right frame of mind for the rest of the movie.

The exposition for *Men in Black* is particularly challenging as it describes an original set-up which requires lengthy explanation. (In case you haven't seen the movie, it is about an American Agency that oversees the aliens who live, for the most part, peacefully among us and who the rest of us know nothing about.) The simpler the situation, the more quickly and easily an audience connects with it, which is why plots about family life, office life, neighbourhood life and so on are so popular.

In *Men in Black* the Agency isn't mentioned at all until 17 minutes into the movie, and the full explanation comes 28 minutes in when a new agent is recruited. By then, of course, the audience should be hooked and willing to sit through a few minutes of explanation.

Looking again at the characters from Chapter 9…

> *The trigger will be the fact that Adam and Laura need to share premises, and the exposition will need to explain how and why this happened. It could be a complicated legal thing, or a simple money-saving exercise for both of them – not a lot of comedy potential there though. What if there was a misunderstanding? That would need a lot of exposition; in fact it would be enough on its own to fill a short piece. Perhaps they could be family, so that one of them felt obliged to let the other one share the office. Perhaps one of them could acquire a share of the other's premises, by inheritance maybe? So, when Laura's partner dies, it's discovered that she's left her share of the House of Relaxation to her nephew Adam. He isn't interested in relaxation, but he does want to use the premises for his own business. This means that Adam isn't related to Laura, so there are no ties of affection to soften their relationship. It also means that I can make some use of the lists and jokes I generated for the 'Funeral Fun' sketch.*

Think about the trigger for your plot, and consider how much exposition is needed.

### CRISES

Constructing a plot consists of taking your characters from the trigger, through a series of crises or obstacles, to a climax followed by a resolution. The crises need to be of increasing severity. It works particularly well if the solution of one crisis is the very thing that gives rise to the next crisis, so that the characters seem to be digging themselves ever deeper into a hole, and are ever closer to total meltdown. The final crisis produces the climax, and after that the plot should move swiftly to the resolution. This basic plot shape of a slow but steadily increasing build-up followed by a quick finale is known as a dramatic arc. It works for all types of writing and all genres.

> *The crises will arise from the mix-up over clients. Perhaps there is only one phone line with clients phoning in for both businesses. Also there may be a shared appointment book, or two books that look identical. If there were two receptionists, one for each business, then Adam and Laura would each have a sidekick. Maybe instead of two books, the New Age business would have an old-fashioned book, but the marketing business would have an electronic system. Adam and Laura each see the wrong client.*

Re-examine your 'What ifs' and rough sequence of events. Make sure there are plenty of crises.

### SUBPLOTS

A substantial piece of storytelling is unlikely to get by with just one plot. A subplot is a smaller story running alongside, and secondary to, the main plot. It can involve minor characters, or can be a series of incidents in the protagonist's life that are less important than the main plot. Of course there can be more than one subplot. It's most satisfying if the subplots are resolved in ways that feed into the resolution of the main plot. This is expertly done in the movie *Little Miss Sunshine*. The main plot is about seven-year-old Olive's desire to enter a beauty pageant, but each of her five older relatives has a subplot.

One function of subplots is that they keep minor characters busy. P. G. Wodehouse said that writers should think of their characters as actors in a play – since they're being paid, they need to be onstage, not just sitting in a dressing room because they've said their one and only line.

> *The two receptionists are an obvious source of a subplot. They could be attracted to each other despite their differences, or they could argue constantly. The mix-up over clients would be their fault. They could fall out over how to arrange the reception area – will it be what Adam wants or what Laura wants? Another subplot could come from the story behind the inheritance – this would incorporate some of the exposition into the plot. Also the two clients could have their own subplot.*

Exercise

Devise one or more subplots.

### ENDINGS

Endings are always important. Whatever you're writing it will be the ending that stays with the audience, creates catharsis or sets them thinking. An ending needs to be both logical and unexpected. Many writers struggle with endings, perhaps because in life there are few complete endings – something always happens next.

There are several types of ending and you need to make a clear choice.

**Closed ending** Just about everything is resolved, particularly in the story of the main characters. For instance, if you end with a wedding or a funeral, then you have taken the story to a natural stopping point. The same is true if the characters are on a quest which is achieved at the end. With this type of ending the characters can never return to the point at which they started – things have changed irrevocably for them.

**Circular ending** The characters do return to the point at which they started. This type of ending is essential in sitcoms, where the characters and their situation must be the same every week. At the same time you do have to resolve the immediate problem that you've set. So you could create a story where a husband and wife have a problem – perhaps they can't decide where to go for their holiday. She wants a beach holiday, he wants an adventure holiday. The problem will have to be resolved by the end – by compromise, or by one of them winning the argument perhaps – but the resolution can't lead to divorce or any other permanent change to the status quo.

**Open ending** An ending which doesn't resolve anything. These are the most difficult to achieve successfully, because audiences on the whole want to know how the story ended – hence the debate about the ending to the original version of *The Italian Job*, still going on after more than 40 years. However in comedy there is more flexibility and open endings can be made to work well. In *The Goon Show* there were quite a few open endings, for instance the episode titled 'The Dreaded Batter-Pudding Hurler (of Bexhill-on-Sea)' has two endings: first listeners are invited to write in with suggestions for the ending and then there is a marriage proposal that has nothing to do with the plot.

### HAPPY OR SAD?

It is not compulsory for a comedy to have a happy ending, although very few have a truly sad ending. The last episode of the sitcom *Blackadder* famously ends with the soldiers going over the top to fight, undoubtedly to be killed. It is extremely powerful and a rare example of a sad ending.

Most writers choose either a happy ending or a mixed ending. If the main character has been selfish or dishonest, or has behaved badly in some other way, then there is a choice as to whether they get away with it at the end or get their comeuppance.

### CONSTRUCTING AN ENDING

If you're constructing a closed or circular ending, then aim for something that is both logical and unexpected. In other words, the audience is unlikely to anticipate the ending, but when it arrives it makes perfect sense. The surprise element should ensure there is a big laugh at the end. Open endings also need to generate a laugh and be unexpected, but by definition aren't logical.

Writers are usually advised to avoid using *deus ex machina* or 'god in the machine' endings. This refers to a habit in ancient Greek drama of ending a story by having the gods intervene. Any kind of supernatural intervention, or introduction of a new factor or character, makes for an unsatisfying ending because it hasn't arisen out of the story.

However in comedy *deus ex machina* endings can work if they are appropriate to the type of comedy. In a conventional sitcom it wouldn't work if, for instance, the couple arguing about the holiday were suddenly given enough money that they could afford both types of holiday. On the other hand *Monty Python* sketches often ended with an unexpected and unexplained intervention, for instance from the Anti-Silliness Patrol.

> *This is a simple story that requires a conventional closed ending to the main plot. The big question is will there be a winner and a loser, two winners or two losers? Anything is possible, but this is my choice:*
>
> *Adam is angry because he has seen the wrong client and lost the business, Laura is smug because she was successful with her client even though it was the wrong one. Then they notice that the receptionists have rearranged the furniture the way Adam wanted. Now Laura is angry, and Adam is smug.*

Exercise

Create an ending for your plot.

---

## Other types of plot

### DIARIES AND LETTERS

One alternative to tightly controlled plotting is to use a looser, more episodic structure. This tends to work best for prose rather than performance and there is a long history of comedy diaries, reaching back to *Diary of a Nobody* in 1888.

Rather than a plot, diaries tend to have a series of running themes. For instance, in *The Timewaster Diaries* by Robin Cooper the dominant theme is his passion for inventing the most bizarre things, along with other themes including his wife constantly spraining her ankle and his Swiss penfriend's frequent puzzling references to 'house handles'. By the end of the year, it looks as if one of the inventions is about to pay off, which is enough of an ending to satisfy the reader.

A variation on the diary idea is letters, seen most recently in *Ladies of Letters* which again is fairly loosely plotted.

### LINKED STORIES

Another approach to plotting, much favoured by P. G. Wodehouse, is to write a series of linked short stories. The same central characters have a series of comic adventures rather like the episodes of a sitcom. And like a sitcom, the individual stories have to be carefully plotted.

---

# Other aspects of plot construction

### THE RULE OF THREE

You've already seen that putting things in threes is a good comedy structure, and this extends to plot construction. The rule of three is excellent for conveying important information. If you can find ways to mention something three times, then you can be sure of getting it across, but do create variety in the ways you mention it.

### SHOW DON'T TELL

This means that character should be revealed through action. It applies particularly to performance, although prose writers need to be aware of it too because too much explanation can make for heavy reading. If two characters don't get on, you can convey that information by having one of them say 'I can't stand X' but it is much more effective to show the hostility between them through an event in the plot.

### REINCORPORATION

You've already seen that reincorporation can work in stand-up routines, and it is also extremely valuable in plotting. Set something up early on, and then don't refer to it again, but use it later on. It can be something that comes back to cause a problem for a character, or it can be used in the resolution. As part of an ending, reincorporation is particularly effective. It creates an ending that is both surprising, because the audience has forgotten about whatever it is, and logical, because it was set up earlier. For example, in the *Absolutely Fabulous* episode 'New Best Friend' about halfway through Eddy's visitors are seen setting up the baby alarm. Then the very last scene uses the alarm, which has been left switched on, to finish the story. The crucial thing is that there is no mention of the alarm at all once it's set up, so the audience forgets about it.

### IRONY

In plot terms irony means that not everyone knows what is going on. Maybe the audience knows something that none of the characters know, or maybe all the characters know except one. *Friends* got a lot of mileage out of the relationship between Chandler and Monica, which the other characters didn't know about but the audience did.

---

## Case history: a plot analysed

Oscar Wilde's enduring comedy *The Importance of Being Earnest* was first performed in 1895 and is still regularly revived.

**Back-story** Jack Worthing was adopted by a wealthy man, now dead. He lives a respectable but dull life in the country which includes being guardian to his adoptive niece Cecily. In order to get away from this and enjoy himself he pretends to have a wild brother called Ernest who lives in London, but Jack himself is actually Ernest. His best friend is Algernon and Jack is in love with Algernon's cousin Gwendolen. Algernon only knows him as Ernest and knows nothing about Jack's other life. Algernon himself has an imaginary friend called Bunbury who he uses as an excuse when he needs to get out of a tedious social event.

**Trigger** Algernon has seen Jack's cigarette case with an inscription to 'Uncle Jack' and has begun to suspect his friend has a double life.

**Plot** Jack tells Algernon he intends to propose to Gwendolen. When challenged about the cigarette case he tells the whole story of his double life but says he is about to give it up as Cecily is far too interested in Ernest.

**First obstacle** Gwendolen accepts Jack's proposal but says that she can only love someone called Ernest – she knows him as Ernest. Jack immediately resolves to change his name and so appears to have an easy solution to this obstacle.

**Second obstacle** Gwendolen's mother, Lady Bracknell quizzes Jack before she can allow the engagement. He does well until he confesses to being adopted, whereupon she rejects him as a suitor and possible husband for her daughter. This is a far bigger obstacle for Jack, and although he doesn't seem to have a complete solution he resolves to announce the death of Ernest to his family in the country, in preparation for changing his own name to Ernest.

Algernon is determined to meet Cecily and so turns up at Jack's home pretending to be Ernest.

**Subplot** It is obvious that Cecily's governess Miss Prism is in love with the local priest, Dr Chasuble.

**Third obstacle** Jack can't tell everyone that Algernon is an impostor because Algernon will reveal Jack's lies. He is obliged to pretend that Algernon is indeed his brother Ernest.

**Subplot** Algernon falls in love with Cecily, proposes and is accepted.

**Fourth obstacle** Cecily announces that she too can only love a man called Ernest. Algernon also decides to have himself christened Ernest.

Gwendolen meets Cecily.

**Fifth obstacle** Gwendolen and Cecily discover they are both engaged to Ernest Worthington. This is quickly resolved when Jack and Algernon turn up and it is clear the women are not both engaged to the same man.

**Sixth obstacle** Gwendolen and Cecily both insist on being engaged to Jack's brother Ernest, not Jack and Algernon. This is resolved when Jack admits he has no brother. Both men persist in the idea of changing their name to Ernest, and Gwendolen and Cecily forgive them.

This plot so far has consisted of a series of obstacles that have been fairly easily resolved, apart from the matter of Lady Bracknell refusing to consider Jack as a suitor for Gwendolen. She won't change her mind unless he makes 'a definite effort to produce at any rate one parent, of either sex, before the season is quite over'. Jack seems to have no answer to this, so it is the main obstacle that the plot hinges on.

**Final crisis** Lady Bracknell consents to the marriage of her nephew Algernon and Cecily when she hears that Cecily is an heiress. Jack seizes his opportunity and, in his role as Cecily's guardian, refuses his permission for the marriage, unless Lady Bracknell also consents to his marriage to Gwendolen. Lady Bracknell refuses and is about to leave. It looks as if all is lost.

This is an important moment. The closer the characters can be taken to the brink of total disaster, the more gripping the plot will be. There is nothing in the play so far to suggest that Jack will find a way to make Lady Bracknell change her mind so he looks to have lost Gwendolen.

**Final twist** Cecily's governess Miss Prism is identified as the woman who abandoned Jack as a baby. This means he can find out something about his parents, in fact he assumes Miss Prism is his mother.

This shows a more appealing side of Jack's rather flippant nature – he isn't bothered about the possibility of his parents being of a lower class and even accepts that he may be illegitimate.

**Resolution** It turns out that Jack is the son of Lady Bracknell's sister and therefore he is Algernon's brother. What's more his real name is Ernest. He is now able to marry Gwendolen, Algernon can marry Cecily and Miss Prism finally captures Dr Chasuble.

The plot is neatly tied up with everyone paired off and no one punished for their past mistakes. It isn't a particularly funny plot, and the laughs are generated by Oscar Wilde's many witticisms. His characters tend to all speak in the same way, but this hasn't stopped the play from becoming a comedy classic. The string of coincidences, and the idea that two young women would have a rather silly fixation with the name Ernest, can only be made to work in a comedy.

## Putting it all together

Once you have a good idea where your plot is going, it's time to start working out the details, and putting the events into some sort of sequence. The considerations will be different depending on whether you've chosen a short story, a sitcom episode or a one-act play. A story can be set anywhere, and move around in time and space, a play is constrained by the physical environment of the theatre and a sitcom by the technical considerations of TV. All forms need a degree of discipline to keep the story within the limited length.

**Back-story** Adam has inherited his Aunt Margaret's share of the House of Relaxation and is moving his own small business into the premises she shared with Laura. Stuart is Laura's receptionist and Wendy is Adam's personal assistant.

**Trigger** Adam and Wendy are moving in. We learn that Stuart and Wendy are not going to get along. Adam is determined to get his own way with Laura – in particular he wants the room that she uses, as Margaret's old room is too small for him.

**Obstacle one** Laura is determined to hang on to her room, and decides to keep it locked. She also uses the excuse that Stuart would never consent to rearranging the Reception area and her room needs to be on the same side as Stuart's desk.

Laura leaves for the Garden Centre, because Margaret said she intended to be reincarnated as a tree. Adam mentions that he has a client due soon, but when Stuart tries to add that to the appointment book Adam shows him their electronic organizer, which speaks the appointments. Stuart is fascinated by the organizer, but has to take a call from a Mr Jamieson asking for an appointment with Laura. Laura returns with a pot plant instead of a tree.

When Stuart is alone, he plays with the organizer and accidentally clears its memory.

**Subplot** Mr Jamieson, a brusque businessman, arrives and is shown into Laura's office.

**Obstacle two** Adam asks Stuart to swap places with Wendy as part of his plan to get Laura's office, but Stuart refuses.

**Subplot** Laura and Mr Jamieson talk at cross purposes.

**Subplot** Another client arrives, as the organizer is blank Adam assumes it is his client.

Adam instructs Wendy to find a way to swap places with Stuart.

**Subplot** Laura's client is beginning to respond to her. Adam's client seems bemused at first but then begins to respond.

Wendy pretends that she can hear Margaret asking to be on Wendy's side of the room so she moves the pot plant, but then pretends that it's set off her hay fever, meaning that she needs to move away from it. The only option is for her to swap places with Stuart.

**Crisis** Both clients are leaving. Laura's client has changed into a New Age type. Adam's client has changed into a businessman but has become so over-confident he doesn't need Adam's help any more. They meet in reception, and it turns out they are father and son who run a family business together.

**Ending** Adam is furious that he's lost the marketing contract, Laura is smug about her success with the businessman. Then they notice that Wendy and Stuart have swapped places. Now Laura is angry and Adam is pleased. Wendy explains that it was all due to Margaret and Laura dumps the pot plant in the waste bin.

Exercise

Work out the detail of your plot.

---

# Editing

In a real-life situation of course you won't work through every single exercise before you start writing. If you're anything like me you'll be inclined to jump straight in and start writing round a rough idea, then realize it isn't working, go back and do some of the prep, then write again, then realize it needs something more, so go back and do some more prep, and so on. This is often quite time-wasting, although sometimes the writing just flows and the prep wasn't needed. You'll work out your own way of doing things, but just remember, if it isn't working, go back to the basic exercises and apply them to the piece you're working on.

**Author insight**

For scripts, I like to make a rough model of the set with a slip of paper for each character, that way I can move them round and make sure my plot hangs together.

At some point do make a step-by-step plan of the plot. Some writers like to do this very early on, while others wait till they've done a rough draft. In either case once you have your plot dissected and laid out in front of you, you'll find it much easier to spot the flaws.

For most types of storytelling, discipline and economy are what's required, so check that every step of the plot is there for a reason, and that it moves the story forward as well as giving information and revealing character. Have a logical reason for everything that happens – but remember that logical is not the same as sensible.

Look at each individual scenario and check that it has its own beginning, middle and cliffhanger before the end. Make sure the ending resolves the main plot, ties up the subplots and focuses on the main character or characters.

*Exercise note: you now have characters and plot for a short piece, but read the next chapter before you write it out.*

## Things to remember

▶ Plots don't have to be funny.

▶ Plots do need conflict and claustrophobia.

▶ Too much claustrophobia reduces the chances for interaction.

▶ Most stories can be seen as a quest for something.

▶ Ask 'What if'.

▶ Keep exposition short if possible.

▶ Create a series of crises.

▶ Use subplots to help with pacing.

▶ Endings can be open, closed, or circular.

# 11

## Sitcoms

In this chapter you will learn:
- *to choose a situation with endless plot possibilities*
- *to create fully developed characters*
- *to create circular plots.*

For many comedy writers a successful TV sitcom is their Holy Grail. There are specific requirements for traditional sitcoms, and in fact very few move outside the basics of the genre.

## Traditional sitcoms

In a traditional sitcom the core situation, sets and characters don't change, except perhaps very slowly in a long-running sitcom. It generally works best if the situation is a believable one that most viewers can identify with, although of course some sitcoms break the rules. For instance, in *Frasier*, while we might believe that Frasier Crane would give a home to his elderly father, the level of the father's disability in no way justifies the services of a full-time live-in physiotherapist.

Most sitcoms are based around no more than three sets or locations which are used in every episode. *The Royle Family* never moved outside the family home (except in various specials) and concentrated on the lounge, the dining area and the kitchen.

The opening episode of any sitcom is always the hardest one to write because it needs to establish the set-up, and the writer can't assume that the audience already knows what it's all about.

## Situation

As we've already seen, just like other types of comedy, sitcoms benefit from a claustrophobic situation. The basic situation for most sitcoms is usually one that will never run out of stories such as a family or a workplace. However even the most carefully chosen situation will be limited by time passing, for instance the young adults who started out flat-sharing in *Friends* were always eventually going to become older people who probably were going to buy houses and have children. Family shows such as *Roseanne, Outnumbered* and *My Family* have to adapt to the fact that the actors playing the children will grow up and move away, often leading to convoluted plot twists to keep them in the family home.

> *Is the situation I've already devised suitable for a sitcom? If Adam and Laura are both unsuccessful running their small businesses, it is feasible that they might share premises indefinitely. Wendy works for Adam because she performs so badly in interviews she can't get another job, and Stuart is too wet to look elsewhere so stays with Laura.*

Exercise

Choose a situation with good sitcom potential. You can use a situation from an earlier exercise.

## Characters

It's been said that sitcoms should be called charactercoms, because it's the characters that matter most. The aim is to put strong well-developed characters into a variety of stories and watch how they cope, always of course staying in character.

Sitcom characters never develop and the longer the series runs, the harder this can be to maintain. It's easier to accept that older characters are set in their ways, which gives sitcoms like *One Foot in the Grave* or *Last of the Summer Wine* a headstart. It's harder to believe that the younger characters from *Coupling* or *Two Pints of Lager and a Packet of Crisps* are still the same several series down the line.

*Gavin and Stacey* is unusual in that it follows the characters through one of life's journeys (i.e. the central characters meet, marry, split up and reunite) but the characters don't change across all three series. This means of course that they never learn anything from their experiences, don't mature or change with the passing of time.

It's also true that sitcom characters, however young, lead routine lives, always going to the same pub and mixing with the same friends. Since this is so unrealistic it can be hard to understand why the format is so enduringly popular – perhaps because we all crave stability and fear change. It also means of course that the characters have to be very strongly conceived from the very beginning, because there's no room for development.

> *Laura is quite a low-profile character, because her essentially selfish drive to get her own way is hidden behind her pretend touchy-feelyness. Adam's flaws are more upfront, since he is clearly deluded about his own success and sex-appeal. Between them there is a lot of potential for laughs. Wendy would need to constantly puncture both Laura's and Adam's pretensions while Stuart would be permanently puzzled by the other three.*

Choose two or three characters for a sitcom. You can use characters from an earlier exercise. Are they strong enough to carry a sitcom? Will you be able to create laughter from their main flaw week after week?

There are two basic formats for sitcom characters:

1 A single point of focus for every episode. Either a single main character surrounded by supporting characters, for example *Miranda*, or a two-hander, such as *Steptoe and Son*.

2 An ensemble, such as *'Allo 'Allo* or *The Thick of It*. All the characters should have some involvement with every episode, but the focus can fall on different characters each week.

*Exercise note: don't attempt to write an ensemble piece just yet – stick with two or three main characters.*

### RELATIONSHIPS

If the characters in a sitcom are fixed, then so too are their relationships. You already know that the characters need to be in conflict and they need binding ties. Once you have these two core factors in place then you can develop the relationships further. When two characters are together, the dynamics are bound to change if a third is brought in to the scene. Look at all the combinations and decide how things will pan out between them.

If you find this difficult, try choosing a model and basing the relationships on it. The family is the easiest model to understand, but you could also use political systems (is this a democracy or a dictatorship?) or the animal world (is this a herd of wildebeest or a pride of lions?).

> *In our story, Laura as the oldest could be a mother figure, albeit a rather selfish one. I see Adam as an annoying brother-in-law, Wendy as a teenager and Stuart as a child. If they were animals in the zoo Laura would be a member of the cat family, small sleek and self-centred, Adam an overly energetic monkey, Wendy a not very poisonous snake and Stuart something lovable but slow, like a koala.*

Exercise

Choose a model for your characters.

---

**Comedy insight – MIRANDA HART**

*The most common mistake that new comedy writers make is, in terms of sitcom, forgetting that story is the most important thing. It might seem fun to write your characters sitting around saying great jokes, but each scene has to go somewhere and move the story on.*

Miranda Hart is a comedy actress and writer

---

# Plots

As you already know, sitcom plots have to be self-contained and circular. The trigger sets the story in motion, and by the end the issues raised by that trigger must be resolved without changing anything about the central situation.

One advantage of writing for a sitcom is that the story can usually start right on the trigger, because the situation and back-stories are given. For example, the *Porridge* episode 'Just Desserts' opens just after the trigger, with Fletcher hunting for his tin of pineapple chunks which has gone missing.

The most effective plots are usually the ones that use the characters' central obsessions. For instance, in *Only Fools and Horses* the plots that focused on Del trying to make money, or Rodney trying to improve himself, were more satisfying than plots about their romantic lives. If you keep the plot simple, it will give the characters room to take over.

It isn't essential to include a subplot in a half hour sitcom. An episode of *Yes Minister* called 'The Greasy Pole' has a plot that runs as straight as an arrow, from the first scene that sets up the need for the Minister to approve a new chemical factory, to the final scene where he finally decides not to approve it. Of course there are twists along the way, but we only get one story.

Mostly though, a subplot helps with both the pacing of the main plot and the suspense, since you can cut to the subplot at crucial moments. In 'Italian for Beginners', an episode of *The IT Crowd*, the main plot is about the mess Jen gets herself into when she pretends to be able to speak fluent Italian, and how Moss helps her. The subplot is about Roy's increasing obsession with his girlfriend's parents, who died in a fire under circumstances that seem to him deeply improbable. The two stories aren't linked and have separate resolutions. You might think that this wouldn't work at all but there are two crucial scenes involving Jen, Moss and Roy in which both the main plot and the subplot are featured, and that is enough to give the episode coherence.

---

**Comedy insight – MINDY GLAZER**

*Sitcoms are not about jokes. They are about character, conflict and action, just like any other good story. Jokes are a way of telling the story. They reveal character, jeopardy and resolution. A sitcom is a story told in jokes the way an opera is a story told in song, but the story comes first.*

Mindy Glazer currently teaches sitcom writing online. She has written for *Who's the Boss*, *Kate and Allie*, and *My Two Dads*, among other shows

---

The only way to find out if your sitcom idea has got enough about it to make a series is to rough out at least six plots.

*In our story, I can see plenty of potential episodes for the House of Relaxation:*

1  Adam and Wendy move in to the House of Relaxation offices.
2  Adam decides the business needs a website, Laura prefers old-fashioned leaflets; they go head to head over it.
3  Laura is having money problems, so decides to write a book about Stress Management.
4  When Adam's flashy car lets him down, he tries to borrow Laura's Beetle but ends up with Stuart's ancient bicycle.
5  Laura decides she's a Druid and bans Christmas, whereas Adam expects to make a whole heap of money with his Christmas marketing ideas.
6  Laura sets up an Alternative Dating Agency.

*And so on.*

**Exercise**

Work out six rough outlines for plots using your situation and characters.

## Putting it all together

In the last few chapters you've created everything you need to write a short comedy piece.

**Exercise**

Write a complete first draft using the material you've generated in the previous exercises. You can write a sitcom episode, or if you prefer a short story or one-act play.

## Things to remember

▶ A situation doesn't have to be completely realistic but should be believable.

▶ Make the situation claustrophobic so the characters are trapped.

▶ Think in terms of three sets.

▶ Relationships between sitcom characters are unchanging.

▶ Sitcom characters lead very routine lives.

▶ Apart from the opener there is very little exposition.

# 12

# Character development and deeper plotting

In this chapter you will learn:
- *about character development*
- *about imagery*
- *about theme, message and emotional impact.*

*Exercise note: the exercises in this chapter are far less detailed than in previous chapters. You already have many of the skills you need, and for this kind of writing you'll benefit from developing your own approach to the work.*

Whenever there's a poll trying to find the world's favourite novel invariably James Joyce's *Ulysses* comes out top. And invariably when pressed most people who vote for it admit they haven't read it, or haven't managed to finish it. This is a shame, because while it is a demanding read, it is also a funny book.

*Ulysses* relies on the comedy technique of bathos. Ulysses, or Odysseus as he was originally known, was the legendary ancient Greek hero who fought in the Trojan War, was involved in the Trojan Horse trick and who then took ten adventurous years to travel back to his home in Ithaca. Joyce's novel on the other hand is about the far from heroic Leopold Bloom and his journey through one day of his life in Dublin in 1904. Joyce uses the Odysseus journey as a template for Bloom's day. He uses comedy in the plot, the characters and the language:

> *The sea, the snotgreen sea, the scrotumtightening sea.*

Any story can be told as either a tragedy or a comedy, and the same themes occur in all forms of storytelling. A man and woman are locked into a bitterly loveless marriage – is this *Who's Afraid of Virginia Woolf*, or *Fawlty Towers*? Or the misery of life in the trenches in World War One – *Birdsong* or *Blackadder*?

### Comedy insight – ALAN AYCKBOURN

*Comedy is, in my opinion, writing that sets out in all seriousness, written from one individual's viewpoint, which other individuals, to his or her mystification, find funny. You can't actually alter the way you view the world. All you can do is write whatever you want to write truthfully and honestly. It's for others to judge whether your viewpoint is 'comic' or 'serious'. If after a few years no one's laughing, don't despair. You may still be a writer but not necessarily a comic one.*

Alan Ayckbourn is a Director and Playwright

Comedy can be a serious literary business. In 2010 a comedy won the Man Booker Prize (*The Finkler Question* by Howard Jacobson). There is nothing to stop you using comedy values to explore deeper issues, either character based or message based (or of course both). However, a writer can't turn any comedy into a serious work just by adding a message or more developed characters – some comedy is far too frothy and fragile for such treatment. You need to feel the urge to write in this way first, and the comedy will develop from that starting point.

## Characters

Serious literary writers usually aim for character development in the main characters. The protagonist is on a journey, and at the end of the story they will have changed in some significant way. Characters such as Raskolnikov and Madame Flaubert are taken through an extreme series of events that have profound effects on them. However not all novels and dramas work this way – protagonists such as Sherlock Holmes and Hercule Poirot don't develop, and their very appeal lies in their consistency.

In comedy the balance is very much in favour of characters like Bertie Wooster that don't develop, and, as we've already seen, in sitcom character development is positively forbidden.

Indeed character development can create problems for a writer. When Nigel Williams wrote *The Wimbledon Poisoner* he tracked his central character, Henry Farr, through something of a midlife crisis and out the other side to a peaceful resolution. However later on, when he had the idea for *Scenes from a Poisoner's Life*, he had to undo a lot of his good work and make Henry unhappy again.

Nevertheless there is character development in some comedy. In *Pride and Prejudice* both the central characters go through a process of learning about their own tendencies to pride and prejudice, and come out of it as more mature people who are ready for married life. In *The Importance of Being Earnest* Jack Worthing has to let go of his hypocritical double life in order to find happiness. In *Men in Black* Will Smith's character Agent J develops from a raw recruit to a fully trained agent. These examples may cover the full spectrum from serious literature to light entertainment but they still have certain basic values in common.

### Exercise

Look back at the work you've already generated and choose one or more characters who have the potential for development.

EXERCISE

#### CONFLICT

Conflict remains crucially important. In *Pride and Prejudice* we meet Elizabeth Bennet just at the moment she is forced to confront a major conflict. She is the right age to marry, and she soon finds there is conflict between her desire to marry for love and the expectations of society and some of her family that she will marry for money and security. She receives a marriage proposal from Mr Collins, who she doesn't love or even like. She refuses him, despite the fact that marrying him would create a secure future for her entire family. This establishes her as a strong-willed and possibly even selfish character who brushes aside conflict with society. Her dealings with other people are rarely conflicted either, since she is naturally assertive and confident.

It is only when she starts to be drawn to Mr Darcy that she suffers internal conflict. She hates him, she turns down his first proposal, she learns the truth about some of his actions, and eventually she faces her own prejudices against him. Her internal conflict and the plot combine together to take her on this journey.

A journey of some sort is the key to a character-based story. In Elizabeth's case it is a journey to enlightenment and a happy ending. The comedy in *Pride and Prejudice* doesn't come from her journey but from other aspects. The large cast of secondary characters are all funny in different ways. Elizabeth herself is witty, in the sparkling style later associated with Oscar Wilde:

> *To find a man agreeable whom one is determined to hate! – Do not wish me such an evil.*

And it's easy to forget, in the light of so many sexually charged adaptations of the book, that Mr Darcy is a ridiculous character in the opening chapters, and is there to be laughed at.

## Messages

In character-based comedy there is always likely to be a happy ending, because the audience will have engaged with the characters and been amused by them. Message-based comedy can often be much darker. The various conflicts in the movie *Dr Strangelove: or how I learned to stop worrying and love the Bomb* are only resolved when the bomb is actually dropped in the last scene, with the implication that the planet is about to be destroyed.

If your writing is message driven, you will still need engaging characters to help the audience connect with the story and its message, although you may not need character development. The black comedy *Slaughterhouse-Five* has a strong anti-war message but the central character is the permanently bewildered and totally non-aggressive Billy Pilgrim. We see the lunacy of war through his eyes. *Catch* 22 uses a more straightforward comedic technique to pursue the same theme, with a central character who doesn't accept the status quo. Yossarian takes the war personally, and constantly asks why people are trying to kill him. Both Billy Pilgrim and Yossarian are versions of the innocent comedy character who sees the world differently from the rest of us.

In *Hard Times* Dickens uses comedy techniques to make his critique of industrial society palatable to an audience who would have been largely either unaware of or indifferent to the sufferings of the industrial poor. However the main characters are not comedy characters at all and there is little character development. Gradgrind and his daughter Louisa do change in the course of the novel, but most of this happens offstage.

Look through the work you've generated so far to see if anything connects with a topic you feel passionately about. The chances are that these issues have already come through in the work you did just to generate laughs.

---

## Plotting

In *Pride and Prejudice* both Elizabeth and Darcy are on a journey that takes them from mutual dislike, through a learning process about their own failings to the destination of love and marriage. That journey isn't possible without the events of the story, and in that sense the plot consists of two elements. The simple business of what happens next is what holds the attention of the audience, but it is the deeper story, the journey of the characters, that creates satisfaction.

The same is true if your piece is message driven. You'll need a plot that carries the audience through the piece and one that also displays your message.

**Comedy insight – SIMON BRETT**

*A lot of people get comedy wrong. They think: 'Wouldn't it be funny if A B C D happened.' A much better starting point is: 'Wouldn't it be tragic if it weren't funny if A B C D happened.'*

Simon Brett is a writer

In *Hard Times* Dickens runs several plots in parallel with inevitable complexity. There are two main plots. One tracks the story of the affluent Gradgrind family, and the complete failure of the Mr Gradgrind's fact-driven system of education which turns his son into a criminal and leads his daughter into a bitterly unhappy marriage.

The other plot follows the desperately hard life of worker Stephen Blackpool and his tragic death.

Not much comedy there, and yet Dickens uses comedy techniques throughout. For instance this is how he sucks the reader into his story. On the first page there is an amusing description of Mr Gradgrind:

*...square wall of a forehead, which had his eyebrows for its base, while his eyes found commodious cellarage in two dark caves, overshadowed by the wall... hair, which bristled on the skirts of his bald head, a plantation of firs to keep the wind from its shining surface, all covered with knobs, like the crust of a plum pie...*

Having introduced Gradgrind, Dickens now wants to show us the miserable place that is his school, where small children become 'little pitchers' to be filled up with facts. But he doesn't want to frighten his readers off at this early stage, so he continues in a humorous vein:

*'Girl number twenty unable to define a horse!' said Mr Gradgrind, for the general behoof of all the little pitchers. 'Girl number twenty possessed of no facts, in reference to one of the commonest of animals!...'*

As the story unfolds comedy takes a back seat, although Dickens is always ready to bring it forward in describing people, and also when he is at his angriest. Here he is describing the reluctance of mill owners to treat their workers decently:

*Surely there never was such fragile china-ware as that of which the millers of Coketown were made. Handle them never so lightly, and they fell to pieces with such ease that you might suspect them of having been flawed before. They were ruined, when they were required to send labouring children to school; they were ruined when inspectors were appointed to look into their works; they were ruined when such inspectors considered it doubtful whether they were quite justified in chopping people up with their machinery; they were utterly undone, when it was hinted that perhaps they need not always make quite so much smoke.*

Note that in the last sentence there is a list of four items, and the third is the most powerful – Dickens using the most basic of comedy techniques.

## SUBPLOTS

Subplots need just as much thought and input as a main plot. The longer and more complex a work the more important subplots become, although they must never overwhelm the main story. The key is to be absolutely sure who your protagonists are and to make sure they are the focus of the main plot, and particularly the ending.

You can use subplots to maintain a comedy tone – as the main stories in *Hard Times* grow darker, Dickens keeps Mrs Sparsit's subplot firmly comedic:

> *...whether she would be plaintive or abusive, tearful or tearing; whether she would break her heart, or break the looking-glass; Mr Bounderby could not at all foresee.*

You can use subplots to expand on the underlying theme of your piece. The main plot has the function of carrying the story forward so is often action driven, whereas in a subplot there is more room for manoeuvre. Joseph Heller uses multiple subplots in *Catch 22* and each one contributes something to the main theme. The death of Snowden is the catalyst for change in Yossarian, the way Orr escapes the war shows that Catch 22 can be beaten and so on.

Exercise

Can any of your existing plot ideas carry the weight of a substantial story? If not, what do you need for this?

---

# Imagery

You've already learnt quite a lot about imagery, which is simply a way of using language to describe one thing in terms of another. Possibly the most well-known image in English is 'I wandered lonely as a cloud'.

Comedy writers play with imagery all the time. If you wrote 'I wandered lonely as the geeky kid with glasses on Sports Day' you'd get two comedy hits, one from playing with a well-known image and one from the new image you've created.

Of course you have the option of creating your own new images. In *Hard Times* Dickens summarized the deeply unnatural nature of industrial life in one memorable image that manages to be both funny and sad at the same time:

> *The piston of the steam-engine worked monotonously up and down, like the head of an elephant in a state of melancholy madness.*

Images become even more effective if they are structured and organized. Dickens adds another animal image by describing the coils of smoke as serpents. And as Stephen Blackpool's story approaches its dreadful crisis he brings the images together:

> *The smoke-serpents were indifferent who was lost or found, who turned out bad or good; the melancholy mad elephants... abated nothing of their set routine, whatever happened.*

### PLOTS AND SUBPLOTS

You can treat your entire plot as an image. This is particularly useful if you are trying to convey a message, however it needs to be subtly done. Allegory, as this type of writing is known, is not as popular as it once was. Audiences now resist being lectured at, although the comedy element may help you slip the message past them.

This was Swift's intention when he wrote *Gulliver's Travels*. Gulliver's journey from one bizarre culture to the next is a progress through the various wickednesses of mankind, and when he finally finds a truly civilized society it is run by horses, with human beings reduced to foul and uncontrollable apes. There is much that's amusing in the story, but the message is as dark as it gets.

### SYMBOLISM

Every time you use an image you're assuming that the audience will bring something to it. Dickens's melancholy mad elephant depends very much on the fondness English readers feel for elephants. After all, we've only seen them in zoos, and have never had our crops trampled or been terrified by a bull elephant on the rampage. A melancholy mad fox would not produce the same effect at all for us.

Symbolism takes this concept even further. The writer deliberately chooses images that they know will have resonance for the audience. *Dr Strangelove* is packed with sexual imagery, from the shots of a plane refuelling in mid-air to the phallic cigars given to the most aggressive characters. The idea behind this is that the same urges that fuel a man's sex drive also fuel the aggression that leads to war.

Decide whether using imagery and symbolism would benefit your piece.

**Author insight**

Sometimes when I'm writing I keep being distracted by irrelevant jokes and ideas. The only cure, for me, is to write them down. Once I had so many extras that I wrote a whole new play with them.

## Theme

If you look at the work you've generated so far you will probably be able to see one or more themes emerging. There is no hiding place for a writer, and once you start to write, your personal obsessions will emerge. After all, these are the things you're interested in, so why wouldn't you write about them? Jane Austen was passionately interested in the tension between love and the pressures on women in her time to marry, and so that is what she wrote about. In the 20th century Kingsley Amis, an equally funny writer, was just as interested in relationships, but he saw everything from a man's point of view.

Sexual politics is a recurring theme of abiding interest to most of us, but you may be far more concerned with global warming or celebrity gossip. There is no point in beating yourself up if your interests seem trivial. If you force yourself to write about deeper issues that don't truly engage you, then your writing will be thin and unconvincing.

Identify any themes that resonate particularly for you.

## Message

Whatever your personal themes are, you will also have an attitude to them. If you're interested in global warming, do you think we're headed for Doomsday or do you think it's a load of fuss about nothing? This is something else you can't fake.

You can choose to write ironically, appearing to support something but all the while quietly undermining it. This was Johnny Speight's intention when he wrote the sitcom *Till Death Us Do Part*. The main character Alf Garnett was held up to ridicule for his outmoded racist and anti-socialist views. Although the series was a huge hit there was much debate at the time as to whether Speight had succeeded, since viewers who agreed with Alf saw him as an embattled man holding out for what was right.

But there's not much we can do about audience reaction to our work. As a writer you have to focus on what you want to say and hope that the message gets through.

EXERCISE

Exercise

Look at each of your themes and decide what your attitude to them is – this will give you your message.

## Theme plus message equals emotional impact

When you put theme and message together then you arrive at the emotional impact of a piece of writing. In *Hard Times* Dickens's themes were his usual one of childhood plus a less usual theme of the Industrial Revolution. His messages briefly put were that young children can be ruined by their early education and that industrial society is an unnatural and soul-destroying way to live. The emotional impact of these is clearly very negative, and as a result Dickens struggles to achieve his usual happy ending.

EXERCISE

Exercise

Examine the emotional impact of your theme and message.

# Things to remember

▶ Comedy can be about character development.

▶ Comedy can be message driven.

▶ Plots function on two levels.

▶ Subplots can carry thematic weight.

▶ Imagery adds another layer.

▶ Imagery can be extended into symbolism.

▶ Emotional impact is created by theme and message.

▶ Emotional impact affects the ending.

# 13

## Editing, polishing and unblocking

In this chapter you will learn:
- *how to edit and polish a draft*
- *to keep going*
- *how to deal with a block*.

Any writer who is satisfied with their first draft is either a fool or a genius. The rest of us have to find the energy for editing, rewriting and polishing. This is true of all forms of writing but comedy writers have an extra problem – once you've read through a piece several times you can lose all sense of how funny it is. All you can do is keep faith with your original vision and carry on with the editing process.

The first thing to do, if the deadline allows, is take a break. Work on something else, do some research or networking for a while, then come back to the piece refreshed. Before you start editing, save the original under a different name. That way you can always come back to it, and knowing that will encourage you to be ruthless.

> ### Comedy insight – SUE LIMB
> *The most common mistake that new comedy writers make is being prickly and possessive about a piece of work and hypersensitive to criticism. Sometimes you just have to throw stuff out and start again.*
> Sue Limb is a comedy writer (Dulcie Domum, *Up the Garden Path*, *The Wordsmiths at Gorsemere*)

We've already looked at editing jokes and editing a sketch, and the same principles apply to editing a longer piece. And here's where the fun really starts, because you'll find that every change you make has a knock-on effect throughout the piece. You'll need to check, check and check again that everything still hangs together after you've finished editing.

# Stages of editing

### READ-THROUGH

Read the piece right through once without stopping before you do any editing, to give yourself an overview, then deal with anything that has leapt out at you as needing attention.

### WRITE TIGHT

Next remove anything irrelevant, and rewrite anything that's too wordy. Pay special attention to your favourite bits. They may be brilliant, but because you like them you'll be reluctant to make changes so try to look at them objectively. If you're writing for performance reduce the directions to the minimum, only keeping those that are crucial. Most of us include far too many directions because as we write we visualize the performance. With prose, only tell your reader what they need to know, as opposed to what you needed to know as the writer. For prose and performance, check that the exposition is both crisp and subtle.

### LOOK DEEP

Once you've done the initial tidy-up you can see the piece much more clearly. Think about your original intentions. You may have done what you set out to do, or you may have ended up with something entirely different, but in either case the writing needs to be consistent. Next look at the theme, message and emotional impact. Check that they hang together and that the ending is appropriate. Even a lightweight piece will have an element of deeper structure so it's worth doing this check.

### BE A DEVIL'S ADVOCATE

Ask as many awkward questions as you can about the plot. Why did it happen this way? Why not another way? Why did he say that, why didn't she do this, what were they thinking of when they did the other? If the answer is just that 'because it's funnier that way' then think again, because it'll be even funnier if you can make everything appear to be entirely logical.

### BE CONSISTENT

Check that characters are consistent at every level – appearance, vocabulary, attitudes, behaviour. Sometimes you choose to make a character inconsistent but you should never let it happen accidentally, or because it suits the plot.

### MARK THE LAUGHS

Whatever you're writing, you need to know where the laughs are. Some types of comedy are more likely to raise a smile than a belly laugh, but you still need to have an understanding of the rhythms of the humour.

> **Comedy insight – KEV F SUTHERLAND**
> *If I had to give just one piece of comedy writing advice it would be to find out if your work is funny. For a stand-up this is easy, you do it in front of people and if they laugh, you're funny. That was where The Sitcom Trials came from, subjecting sitcom writing to the same test a stand-up has to go through, letting the audience tell you what works and what doesn't. For my comic strip work it is harder, and it's quite possible I've never had feedback telling me how funny my comic strips are. Gulp. Maybe they're not?*
>
> Kev F Sutherland is a comedian and comic artist (*Beano, Marvel, Viz*, etc.)

EXERCISE

Exercise

Edit the one-act play, short story or sitcom episode you wrote earlier.

---

## How easy was that then?

I suspect I've made the whole writing process sound pretty easy. A few lists, a bit of lateral thinking, some writing and editing and hey presto, you're a comedy writer. If it was that easy, wouldn't everyone be doing it? At every stage you can find yourself struggling for one reason or another and there will always be times when only willpower, or obsession, will keep you going.

> **Comedy insight – CHRIS RITCHIE**
> *Work hard. No one gets an easy ride in comedy. You have to put in the hours. It takes a lot of trial and error. If you want to write comedy it helps to see first hand how it goes over in a live context. The problem with writing is that you aren't talking to anyone and you cannot predict how funny it is going to be, if at all. When your*

## TIME

Creative writing takes a particular kind of stamina. Like any other project, you start in a rush of enthusiasm but can simply run out of steam after a while. It's important to keep going at these times, even if progress is slow. It can help to have a writing routine, with specific times set aside for getting down to it. Some writers like to create a timetable, so they know when they're due to finish the first draft, or they have a deadline for a certain number of words. Breaking the task down into small achievable units can help, so that you have a sense of progress as each one is ticked off.

It takes most writers between two weeks and a month to write a half-hour sitcom episode. Many novelists think in terms of two years for a novel. If you're realistic about the timescale, you're less likely to become disheartened and give up.

### Author insight

One way of increasing your productivity is this: never end a writing session on a full stop. Always leave something that will help you get started quickly next time – the first sentence of the next bit, or some notes about it.

### BLOCKAGE

Is writer's block an urban myth? Surely if you want to write, then you'll just do it, won't you? Well, maybe, just like people who want to get fitter join a gym, and then never go there. We all fantasize about the wonderful things we're going to do in the future, and then give up when we find out how difficult it gets. That's one explanation for writer's block, and only you can decide whether to tough it out or give up.

Another may be that, for whatever reason, you just don't want to write the next bit. If that's the case, make brief notes for it and move on to something else. There's no rule that says the writing process has to be linear. This kind of block is often caused by your mind focusing on another part of the work that you really want to write.

Once you've got that out of the way, there's a good chance the block will be gone.

Sometimes you can feel blocked because you're trying to think about too many things at once. Take a moment to clear your mind of anything that isn't relevant to the next few sentences, whether they're connected with your writing project or with your life outside writing.

> **Author insight**
> If you find your mind is crowded with all sorts of other concerns then write them down as a list. You might even need two lists: a To Do list and a To Worry About list.

Writing is a solitary business and sometimes it helps to share things with other writers. Having contact with people who understand your difficulties and frustrations is always helpful, and if you're lucky you'll find their enthusiasm and excitement is contagious. Phone, email or meet up with your writing friends as a way of kick-starting your writing.

## Things to remember

▶ The work won't seem funny after several read-throughs.

▶ Take a break and come back refreshed.

▶ Tighten the writing at every level.

▶ Re-examine the deeper aspects of the piece.

▶ Ask awkward questions.

▶ Count the laughs.

▶ Don't panic if you feel blocked.

# Part two
# Information

# 14

## Comedy formats

In this chapter you will learn:
- *about formats for short jokes*
- *about shaggy dog stories*
- *about rhyme patterns.*

**Comedy insight – CANDY GUARD**
> *The most common mistake that new comedy writers make is telling lies.*

Candy Guard is a comic artist (*Pond Life*, the *Observer*)

There are a lot of formats for jokes and comedy generally. They provide a framework for the writer and an expectation for the listener.

## Short formats

We've already looked at 'changing a lightbulb' jokes and 'going into a bar' jokes in Chapter 6. Here are a few more formats for short jokes with examples:

**Knock-knock**

> 'Knock knock.'
> 'Who's there?'
> 'Norma Lee.'
> 'Norma Lee who?'
> 'Norma Lee I have my key.'

**Doctor doctor**

> *'Doctor doctor, I feel like a pack of cards.'*
> *'Wait there and I'll deal with you later.'*

**Waiter**

> *'Waiter what's this fly doing in my soup?'*
> *'Breaststroke?'*

**Confucius says**

> *'Man who tell too many lightbulb jokes soon burn out.'*

**Murphy's Law**

> *If everything seems to be going well, you must have overlooked something.*

**What's the difference?**

> *What's the difference between roast beef and pea soup?*
> *Anyone can roast beef but no one can pee soup.*

**What do you get if you cross…**

> *What do you get if you cross a tourist and an elephant?*
> *Something that carries its own trunk*

---

## Shaggy dog stories

The idea of a shaggy dog story is to make the joke as long as possible (a four-hour car journey gives the lover of shaggy dogs an ideal opportunity) and in its purest form the shaggy dog has no punchline at all, it just reaches an anticlimax and stops. The classic joke of this form is about a man who buys a dog that is very shaggy, and everyone he speaks to agrees that the dog is the shaggiest they've ever seen (and this list of people can go on for ever) until the very last person says 'it isn't that shaggy' and the joke ends.

While your friends and family may be extremely tolerant of this type of joke, in a professional situation it's a risky strategy that depends very much on the performer. Another type of shaggy dog, that leads to an unexpected and ridiculous pun, has a better chance of success.

*A man was famous for the wonderful tulips that he grew. People used to come from all over just to admire them and to try and get the secret of how he grew them. No one could discover just what it was that turned ordinary bulbs into the most beautiful tulips. One day his friend decided that he would get the secret out of him. He went round one evening with a few bottles of wine and as the tulip grower got drunker and drunker, the friend gradually turned the conversation around to tulip growing. Eventually the tulip grower started to explain how he did it.*

*And this is what he said. 'You know my farm is overrun with rodents, thousands of them. I lay traps everywhere to catch them; if I didn't do that all the tulip bulbs would get eaten before they could flower. But then I've got all these little dead bodies to dispose of, so I cook them up and turn them into jam. But then no one will eat the jam, so I spread it on the fields. And it must be wonderful stuff, because it makes the tulips grow like anything.*

*And his friend said, 'You know what, I don't believe a word of it. Tell me what you really do.' And the tulip grower said, 'Oh yeah? Everyone knows you get Tulips From Hamster Jam.'*

---

## Other formats

### CONUNDRUMS

In its narrowest meaning a conundrum is a verbal puzzle that involves a pun:

> *What is black and white and red all over? A newspaper. (red/read)*

but it can also play with an idiom:

> *Why don't cannibals eat clowns? Because they taste funny.*

In its broader sense a conundrum can be any kind of puzzle where the answer requires a degree of lateral thinking and isn't even necessarily funny:

> *Every day a man leaves his apartment on the 46th floor and rides the lift down to the first floor to go to work. Every evening*

> *he takes the lift up to the 38th floor, gets out and walks up the stairs for the remaining eight floors until he reaches the 46th floor. Why? Because he is too short to reach the lift buttons above 38.*

And sometimes a conundrum is a question without an answer:

> *Why are boxing rings square?*

These kind of questions are staple for stand-up comics, often in this rather tired format:

> *If you want to turn off your computer, you have to press the start button. What's that all about then?*

## SPOONERISMS

These are named after the Rev Spooner, a 19th-century cleric. He was teased for inadvertently swapping the initial letters of words to comic effect, although there is little evidence that he actually did so. For example:

> *'Well boiled icicle' for 'well oiled bicycle'*

And one splendid set of three sentences:

> *You have hissed all my mystery lectures. You have tasted a whole worm. Please leave Oxford on the next town drain. (You have missed all my history lectures. You have wasted a whole term. Please leave Oxford on the next down train.)*

More complicated Spoonerisms play with syllables and entire words, such as

> *I'd rather have a bottle in front of me than a frontal lobotomy.*

Occasionally this trick provides material for a cleverly written sketch – Benny Hill and the Two Ronnies both used it. It can also help convey obscenity without actually using the taboo words.

## MALAPROPISMS

These are named after the character Mrs Malaprop from Sheridan's play, *The Rivals*. She consistently uses words inappropriately, such as 'pineapple' instead of 'pinnacle'. More recently George Bush has given comedians masses of similar material with his inability to find the right word, or even a real word:

> *'They misunderestimated me.'*

Steve Delaney continues this type of comedy with his character Count Arthur Strong who gets in a terrible muddle with words.

### TOM SWIFTIES

Tom Swifties started as a parody of a style used in a series of books from the early 20th century. The idea is to use an adverb in a punning way:

> *'We must put the fire out,' he said heatedly.*

> *'I twisted a muscle,' he said limply.*

Sometimes you can get another layer with a pun in the adverb:

> *'I hear Elvis is dead,' she said expressly (Ex-Presley).*

There are many variations on this basic theme, not all using adverbs:

> *'Mmm, a burger in a bun,' she said with relish.*

Tom Swifties may seem too specialized to bother with, but writing them is another good way of training up your comedy muscles. The basic jokes can sometimes be used to add texture to a comedy scenario. For instance if you were writing about a disastrous barbecue you might find a use for 'heatedly' and 'with relish', especially if you had a character who was known for their feeble jokes.

### LIMERICKS

Limericks are simple five-line poems using an AABBA rhyme pattern. (This just means that all the 'A' lines must rhyme with each other and the 'B' lines must rhyme with each other). The first line is usually about the name of the subject or where they live.

> *There once was a woman from Ryde*
> *Who ate some green apples and died.*
> *The apples fermented*
> *Inside the lamented*
> *And made cider inside her insides.*

## CLERIHEWS

The clerihew was invented by Edmund Clerihew Bentley. It consists of a four-line verse with the rhyme pattern AABB. Usually the first line includes the subject's name and the third and fourth lines are longer than the first two – this irregularity adds to the comic effect.

> *Lesley Bown*
> *Tried to write it all down*
> *But when she needed a rhyme for clerihew*
> *She found that there were very few.*

---

## Things to remember

▶ There are many formats for short jokes.

▶ Shaggy dog stories are difficult to pull off in stand-up.

▶ Limericks and clerihews follow pre-set rhyme patterns.

# 15

## Figures of speech

In this chapter you will learn:
- *about figures of speech in comedy.*

**Comedy insight – JAN ETHERINGTON**

*It is very hard for new comedy writers to hang on to their vision, their original idea, their words and their sanity, because many people will offer an opinion of your work and very little of it will be constructive, or even right. Comedy writers are not trusted to know what's funny, because everyone thinks they have funny bones. Keep your sense of humour – but keep a hit list!*

Jan Etherington is an award-winning comedy writer, broadcaster and journalist

The various ways of using language known as figures of speech can almost all be used to create comedy. Remember that wordplay jokes on their own usually raise no more than a smile, but they have their place and can add texture to comedy writing.

There are too many figures of speech to list all of them, so here are a few of the most useful (and don't worry if the names are unfamiliar, I had to look them up too).

**Alliteration** Using the same initial letter for a series of words, as used in tongue twisters. If you're writing scripts, be careful that you don't include accidental tongue twisters that the actors might struggle to cope with, although anything sayable might generate a laugh. Here's Adam trying to fit in a client:

> *Wendy, check if I've got a window on Wednesday.*

**Anthropomorphism and zoomorphism** Anthropomorphism means describing animals in human terms. There is a lot of fun to be had off the person who claims that a particularly dumb pet dog 'understands every word you say' and a somewhat crueller laugh to be had if they say that about another person. Zoomorphism means describing humans in animal terms, for example 'as strong as an ox'.

**Euphemism** This is using an acceptable term instead of one that might be considered too blunt or offensive. Most euphemisms are, understandably enough, around sex and bodily functions. There are many ways to use them to get laughs including the very old but still roadworthy trick of decoding the truth behind adverts and jargon. For instance, here is part of a list decoding job advert euphemisms:

> **Apply in person:** *if you're old, fat or ugly you'll be told the position has been filled.*

> **Competitive salary:** *we remain competitive by paying less than our competitors.*

> **Duties will vary:** *anyone in the office can boss you around.*

> **Join our fast-paced company:** *we have no time to train you.*

> **Must have an eye for detail:** *we have no quality control.*

> **Seeking candidates with a wide variety of experience:** *you'll need it to replace three people who just left.*

**Homonyms and homophones** Homonyms share the same spelling and pronunciation but have different meanings, such as *rose* (the flower) and *rose* (stood up). Words that have the same sound but different spellings, such as *tale* and *tail*, are called homophones and are used to create puns (see later). Clearly how you use them will depend on whether you're writing for the page or for performance. One can imagine having fun with the words carrot and carat, mixing up vegetables and diamond rings, but only in performance. An extension of this principle using more than one word led to the classic Two Ronnies fork handles/four candles sketch.

**Irony and sarcasm** Essentially irony is saying one thing when you mean another, and so is closely linked to sarcasm. Both are comedy staples. They are often conveyed by tone of voice, so if someone is asked to help with the housework, and they reply 'oh yes I'd love to help' there is no way of knowing they are being sarcastic unless there is an indication in the text. Their meaning is crystal clear however if they say 'oh yes, I'd love to help, just about as much as I'd love to jump into a vat of boiling tar.'

The speaker here is being intentionally ironic, but another type of irony occurs when the speaker is unaware of the irony behind their words. So they might offer to help with the housework not realizing that the house in question has just burned down.

**Litotes** Litotes is the odd trick of creating a positive statement by using negatives, such as 'I'm not entirely convinced you're right about that' as a way of saying 'I think you're wrong.'

**Pathetic fallacy** This is giving human characteristics to inanimate objects. In literature this usually refers to nature, so that for instance characters imagine the weather reflects their mood. To make this funny, it needs to be very obviously inappropriate, for instance when Basil Fawlty loses his temper with his car, he addresses it as 'you' and says he's going to give it 'a damn good thrashing'.

**Puns** A pun is a play on words. It can be based on a word that has more than one meaning:

> *The duck said to the bartender, 'put it on my bill'.*

or different words that have the same pronunciation

> *Seven days without food make one weak. (one week)*

The concept can be extended to two or more words:

> *It is better to have loved a short person and lost, than never to have loved a tall.*

**Metonymy and synecdoche** Metonymy means using an associated word rather than the actual name of something, for instance journalists will often use 'Whitehall' to stand for the Civil Service, and car drivers will say 'I broke down' when they mean that the car broke down. Synecdoche means using the name of a part of something to refer to the whole thing, such as when workers are called 'hands', and also using the whole of something to refer to the part, such as 'the whole world was against him' meaning just a part of the world was against him. Dickens uses synecdoche to humorous effect in *Hard Times*:

> *Lady Scadgers (an immensely fat old woman, with an inordinate appetite for butcher's meat, and a mysterious leg which had now refused to get out of bed for fourteen years)...*

**Synonyms and antonyms** Synonyms are words that mean the same as each other, although usually there is a subtle difference in meaning. If a word has more than one meaning it's likely to have more than one synonym – for instance *lie* can mean *deceive, recline* or *be located*. Antonyms are opposites, or near opposites, and again the more meanings a word has the more antonyms it will have. Moving between the meanings is a simple way of surprising an audience.

**Zeugma and syllepsis** Zeugma is using one verb for two actions:

> *He kissed her on her forehead, she on his cheek.*

Syllepsis is similar, but the two actions are not compatible, and therefore funnier:

> *She walked out of the house and into his heart.*

Clearly the more incongruous the two actions, the funnier the effect.

---

## Things to remember

▶ Performers may struggle with tongue twisters.

▶ Irony and sarcasm are comedy staples.

▶ Wordplay jokes are not enough on their own.

# 16

## Comedy styles and genres

In this chapter you will learn:
- *about different styles of comedy*
- *about different genres*.

There are many different ways of making people laugh, and comedy can be divided in various ways into styles and genres. They tend to overlap and most comedy works fall into more than one category. In the same way writers and performers will often work with more than one type of comedy. You will already have your own preferences and an instinct for the type of comedy you want to write, but an understanding of the different categories will help you when you're trying to place your work.

> **Comedy insight – ALAN AYCKBOURN**
> *The most common mistake that new comedy writers make is trying to be funny.*
>
> Alan Ayckbourn is a Director and Playwright

> **Comedy insight – RAY COONEY**
> *The most common mistake that new comedy writers make is trying to be funny.*
>
> Ray Cooney is a playwright

## Types of comedy

### ALTERNATIVE

This usually refers specifically to the comedy of the 1980s, which was more political than the mainstream comedy of the time and wasn't joke based.

### BLACK COMEDY

Black comedy deals with difficult and disturbing subjects such as death and war. *The League of Gentlemen* and *Psychoville* are recent TV examples which aim to make you laugh while simultaneously sending a shiver down your spine. Some black comedy has a deeply serious aim, for instance Kurt Vonnegut's anti-war novel *Slaughterhouse-Five*.

### BLUE COMEDY

This term comes from the music hall comedian Max Miller, who kept all his naughty jokes in a blue notebook. It mostly refers to jokes about sex and bodily functions, but can also include profanity, swearing and anything else likely to shock that particular audience. Live performance is always far more extreme than TV, movie or radio. Some performers have two acts, keeping the bluer one for their live appearances, while others, like Jethro and Roy 'Chubby' Brown confine themselves to live work.

### BURLESQUE

Burlesque is a form of theatrical comedy which started as a combination of sexual come-on and parody of opera and classical theatre. In the buttoned-up Victorian era the scantily dressed women offered audiences something truly exciting, and burlesque challenged mainstream standards. It was hugely popular as a result but disappeared in the late 20th century. Recently there's been something of a revival, although burlesque no longer offers a titillating contrast with the mainstream.

### CARICATURE AND IMPRESSIONS

Both of these involve picking up on the traits of a real, well-known person and exaggerating them to get laughs. Caricatures are more extreme and less realistic than impressions. Satirists use both to make serious points.

### CHARACTER COMEDY

Just as it sounds, character comedy derives humour from the characters' behaviours and reactions. It is the driving force of sitcom and much other comedy.

### CROSSOVER

Crossover takes characters from one comedy and moves them into another. Frasier Crane was a minor character in *Cheers* but was moved into *Frasier* as the main character. Characters can also make occasional appearances – Sam Malone, the central character from *Cheers* was written into one episode of *Frasier*. The term crossover is sometimes mistakenly used to describe comedy drama.

### DEADPAN

As mentioned in Chapter 7 deadpan comedians keep a straight face whatever happens.

### HIGH AND LOW

These rather old-fashioned terms still have some relevance, because there is still a certain amount of snobbery that tends to discount low comedy. Low comedy includes most physical comedy, silly jokes, horseplay and so on. High comedy is more cerebral although it's worth noting that to be successful it often needs to include elements of low comedy – *Monty Python's Flying Circus* is a good example of this.

### IMPROVISATIONAL COMEDY

Mike Leigh has been using improvisation to create scripts since the 1970s. In recent years stand-up comedians developed an improv approach, starting in comedy clubs and then moving into TV via radio. Initially only short pieces were improvised, for instance in the 1980s show *Whose Line Is It Anyway?* Recently there have been improvised sitcoms, including the US show *Curb Your Enthusiasm* and the UK's *Getting On*. Inevitably the performers also get the writing credits.

### IRONY

See Chapter 15.

### MOCKUMENTARY

This portmanteau word means 'mock documentary'. It's a type of parody and currently popular in TV and movie comedy. The key is to use the conventions of the documentary form but undermine them in some way. For instance *The Office* creates an entire fictional world in the style of a documentary, whereas Sacha Baron Cohen takes his fictional characters out into the real world.

### MUSIC-BASED COMEDY

This covers a wide range of possibilities, including parodies of popular songs, new lyrics for old songs and so on. Not to be confused with musical comedy, a theatre genre which is entertaining but not usually funny.

### OBSERVATIONAL COMEDY

See Chapter 6.

### PARODY

Parody is also called send-up, spoof or lampoon. The aim is to take an established piece of work or a performance and create a new version that highlights and exaggerates its features to the point of absurdity. Impressionists inevitably use parody related to the subject of the impression.

It goes without saying that the target of the parody needs to be well-known to the audience. When Jane Austen parodied Gothic novels in her early novel *Northanger Abbey* she was picking on a popular format. Being the subject of a parody could be seen as a mark of success.

### SATIRE

Satire aims to point out the shortcomings of society, organizations and individuals by ridiculing them. Satirical writers often have a desire to force change, and so it is comedy with a purpose, and often quite short-lived because of its topical nature. However some satire survives, for instance Aldous Huxley's *Brave New World*.

Irony, parody and sarcasm are all useful tools of the satirist's trade. Panel shows such as *The News Quiz* on Radio 4 and *Have I Got News For You* on BBC TV are predominantly satirical.

If you're writing satire you need a strongly developed sense of how far to go. It's easy to alienate an audience by overdoing the satire – the last thing you want is to create sympathy for your target. Equally you need to be sure the audience will understand that you're being satirical. In 2001 the 'Paedophile Special' of the series *Brass Eye* caused an uproar, but arguably missed its target, which apparently was media witch-hunts rather than paedophiles.

Political satire uses comedy with serious intent but the prime requirement for it is to be funny. As Peter Cook pointed out the fashion for satire in 1930s Berlin had little effect on the rise of Hitler.

### SLAPSTICK

Slapstick is a type of physical comedy involving cartoon-like violence and extreme behaviours. It's been around for a very long time but we never seem to tire of it. Charlie Chaplin and Buster Keaton took slapstick into the movies and many comedy movies are still essentially slapstick: *Airplane, Spaceballs, AceVentura Pet Detective, Mask, Home Alone, Naked Gun* and so on.

### SURREAL COMEDY

Surreal comedy is connected to the surrealist movement in art but actually predates it, since Lewis Carroll's humour is surreal. Surreal comedy is bizarre and absurd, but there is still a degree of internal logic. *The Goon Show* was the first popular surreal comedy, and *Monty Python* brought the genre to TV. More recently *The Mighty Boosh* are carrying on the tradition. It's difficult to write unless you have a natural tendency in that direction and most of the writers are also performers.

### TOPICAL COMEDY

Doing exactly what it says on the tin, topical comedy relies on news and current affairs as its source material. Writers have to be very quick off the mark and get the material out there while the news items are still hot.

> **Comedy insight – MIKE VARDY**
> *The most common mistake that new comedy writers make is trying to make established characters fit a plot that is unsuitable for them.*
>
> Mike Vardy is a TV director

## Genres

### COMEDY DRAMA

Comedy drama mixes comedy with drama in roughly equal proportions. Some people feel that trying to do two things means you end up doing neither of them well, but there is a sizeable audience for it. When it's done well the drama element drives the plot forward while the comedy keeps the audience entertained. Theatre and movie comedy dramas tend to be one-off stories, while on TV it is more likely to be a filmed series. At one time this would consist of a story told over several episodes (such as *The Beiderbecke Trilogy*) but recently US TV companies have found a winning formula for ongoing soap opera type comedy dramas such as *Glee, Desperate Housewives* and *Ugly Betty*.

### COMEDY OF MANNERS

This is a form of satire that focuses on the affectations of a particular social class. Although its heyday was in the 17th century, Oscar Wilde and Noël Coward continued the tradition. Witty dialogue is essential, along with a plot that revolves round breaking a social taboo.

### COMEDY THRILLER

This is a popular movie and novel genre that's been around for a while – the classic *The Thin Man* was made in 1934. Usually these movies are action based and avoid the graphic violence of many straight thrillers, but not always – *Grosse Point Blank* utilized comedy values but is about a cold-blooded killer. Carl Hiaasen combines comedy thrillers with environmental concerns in his novels.

### FARCE

Farce started as a theatre genre characterized by a fast-moving plot full of unlikely situations, misunderstandings, disguises and hidden agendas. Generally there is a central protagonist with something to hide and the plot hinges on their increasing desperation. There is usually a happy ending, although this isn't obligatory. It has been unpopular in recent years and is seen as rather unsophisticated. However elements of farce appear in many sitcoms, movies and stage plays.

### ROMANTIC COMEDY

Romantic comedy, or romcom, is a genre in which two apparently unsuited people are eventually united for a happy ending. Jane Austen is the first romcom novelist. Movie examples are *It Happened One Night* (1924) and *Love Actually* (2003). TV series such as *Ugly Betty* and *Gavin and Stacey* use the same conventions but rarely reach an entirely happy ending since the makers are generally hoping for another series.

A serious piece that uses comedy to lighten the mood or to throw the sad aspects of the story into sharp contrast. There doesn't necessarily have to be a happy ending, and tragicomedy lends itself to a mixed or ironic ending. Alan Ayckbourn and Mike Leigh have both specialized in tragicomedies.

## Things to remember

▶ Categories are not absolute and often overlap.

▶ Black comedy often has a serious intention.

▶ Targets for parody and satire need to be well-known to the audience.

# 17

Writing for different media

In this chapter you will learn:
- **about writing for recorded performance**
- **about writing for live performance**
- **about writing for print media**
- **about writing for the Internet**.

*Note: This chapter gives some brief guidelines about various media and refers you to other books in the Teach Yourself series that go into greater detail.*

You probably already know what sort of comedy you want to write, and for which medium. Perhaps you can already see yourself collecting your BAFTA, Man Booker Prize or Oscar. But have you given any thought to the specific requirements of each type of comedy writing? There is a certain amount of crossover, and the more successful you are, the more likely it is that your sitcom will move from TV to radio (or vice versa), your novel will be filmed, or your journalism be published in book form.

At the beginning of your career you'll almost certainly have a lot more rejection than success, but once you've sent a piece to every possible outlet then consider rewriting it, or rejigging the original idea for a different medium. This gives you a whole new set of opportunities. However don't rush into this – get to know your chosen medium in depth first and then branch out.

From a writer's perspective many of the differences between media are technical, but we should also bear in mind the idea that 'the medium is the message'. This concept was first floated in the 1960s by Marshall McLuhan and, sidestepping the ongoing philosophical debate about it, we can take it to mean that the medium influences how the message is perceived. How often have you been disappointed by the movie of your favourite book? Or bought a book based on a TV series and been equally disappointed? That happens because in the transition from one medium to another something is lost. Other things may be gained, but the end result is different and will be experienced differently by the audience.

Every now and then though it does work, and that's because the writer and anyone else involved were sensitive to the differences between the two media concerned (the musical *Mamma Mia* and the movie version are an excellent example of a successful transition). All of this is as true for comedy as for any other type of writing.

**Comedy insight – KEN ROCK**

*The most common mistake that new comedy writers make is thinking their work cannot be altered to suit other formats. It can. Also, don't think there are only one or two markets to send your work to. There are many markets that accept new writers. You have to find them. They won't come to you.*

Ken Rock is President of the British Society of Comedy Writers

## Example

Some years ago I wrote a stage play with Ann Gawthorpe that was packed with characters and incident. We decided it had the makings of a novel and so we created a new, longer plot. Here's an extract:

*As soon as Hermione stomped out of the hall and Joyce left to find her tourists something strange happened to the suit of armour. It appeared to come to life. It creaked, moved and swore.*

*'Damn,' it said, 'dropped it.' There was a certain amount of scuffling about and then the musical tones of a mobile phone being dialled.*

*'Hello? Betting World? This is Savile Kingsford.'*

*The suit of armour was a fake. Far from being medieval, it was designed in the 1950s as a cocktail cabinet. The late lamented butler had removed the shelves, the bottle holders and the music box that played Greensleeves, added a strategic dent and*

*successfully passed the thing off as medieval. As the whole of the back was hinged it had become Savile's favourite hiding place. Unfortunately Joyce, in her distraction, was taking the tour backwards and Savile was no longer alone.*

*'… and if you would like to follow me now,' she was saying, 'we will go into the main hall, and here as you can see, we have all the family portraits, starting with Sir Richard Kingsford, 1358 to 1418, who built the manor, right up to the present-day owner Lady Hermione, pictured here in her debutante's ballgown.' The tourists followed her, unimpressed.*

*'The other main feature of the hall is the family collection of armour,' she went on. 'Over here we have the suit worn by Sir Brawdly Kingsford at the battle of Agincourt. And here you can see the dent where the fatal arrow struck him in the codpiece.'*

*'No, don't put me on hold,' said the suit of armour, 'I need to talk to Stibbs…'*

*Joyce nearly jumped out of her skin. Fortunately, the tourists were all Japanese and they assumed that talking armour was just some electronic gadget.*

*'Oh Mr Savile,' Joyce said, 'I didn't see you there.' There was a loud clang as Savile banged his head and a smaller one as he dropped his phone again.*

*'Oh, Joyce, is that you, I was, um, just checking it for rust.'*

We then realized that the new plot would work on TV, although it meant losing a lot of the detail we'd enjoyed putting into the novel. In this extract the audience already knows that Savile needs a quiet place to make his surreptitious phonecall to the bookmaker:

*SCENE 4. INTERIOR. STONE FLAGGED HALL. DAY*

*[THREE WALLS ARE COVERED IN PORTRAITS; THE OTHER HAS PIKES, SWORDS AND SHIELDS ON IT. AROUND THE ROOM ARE FULL-SIZED SUITS OF ARMOUR. JOYCE IS STANDING SURROUNDED BY TOURISTS. SHE IS INDICATING ONE OF THE PORTRAITS.]*

> JOYCE:    *...and here as you can see, we have all the family portraits, starting with Sir Richard Kingsford, 1358 to 1418, who built the manor, right up to the present-day owner Lady Hermione, pictured here in her debutante's ballgown.*

*[THE CAMERA ZOOMS IN ON ONE OF THE SUITS OF ARMOUR. WE HEAR A MOBILE PHONE BEING DIALLED]*

SAVILE:   *(WHISPERING) Hello? This is Savile Kingsford.*

*[JOYCE FOLLOWED BY THE TOURISTS MOVES ACROSS TO THE SUIT OF ARMOUR]*

> JOYCE:    *The other main feature of the hall is the family collection of armour. Over here we have the suit worn by Sir Brawdly Kingsford at the Battle of Agincourt. And here you can see the dent where the fatal arrow struck him in the codpiece.*

SAVILE:   *(WHISPERING) No, don't put me on hold.*

*[JOYCE AND THE TOURISTS REACT IN AMAZEMENT]*

SAVILE:   *(WHISPERING LOUDER) I said don't put me on hold.*

TOURIST #1:   *Is it haunted?*

*[JOYCE TAPS LOUDLY ON THE ARMOUR. WE HEAR THE SOUND OF A MOBILE PHONE BEING DROPPED INSIDE A SUIT OF ARMOUR]*

SAVILE:   *Ouch! What, who's there?*

*[SAVILE LIFTS UP THE VISOR AND PEERS OUT]*

JOYCE:   *Mr Savile!*

SAVILE:   *I was, um, just checking it for rust, Joyce.*

It didn't seem too much of a jump to turn the TV script into a radio script, although this particular scene gave us a few problems. Even though the phonecall to the bookie has been set up, will the audience actually twig that Savile is inside the suit of armour?

*SCENE 4 INT. MORNING*

*ATMOS:   STONE FLAGGED HALL*

*F/X:*   PEOPLE MURMURING (UNDER), FOOTSTEPS

*JOYCE:*   *And if you would like to follow me now, we will go into the main hall, and here as you can see, we have all the family portraits, starting with Sir Richard Kingsford, 1358 to 1418, who built the manor, right up to the present-day owner Lady Hermione, pictured here in her debutante's ballgown.*

*F/X:*   PEOPLE MURMURING (UNDER) MOBILE PHONE DIALLING INSIDE A SUIT OF ARMOUR

*SAV:*   *(WHISPERING) Hello? Betting World? This is Savile Kingsford.*

*JOYCE:*   *The other main feature of the hall is the family collection of armour. Over here we have the suit worn by Sir Brawdly Kingsford at the Battle of Agincourt. And here you can see the dent where the fatal arrow struck him in the codpiece.*

*SAV:*   *(WHISPERING) No, don't put me on hold again. Just tell me whether Burdock collected my winnings, sorry, his winnings?*

*F/X:*   PIECE OF ARMOUR DROPPING ON FLAGSTONE

*JOYCE:*   *Oh, Mr Savile, I didn't see you in there.*

*SAV:*   *(WHISPERING) So who was it that picked them up?*

*JOYCE:*   *Er… would you like us to come back when you've finished your phonecall?*

*F/X:*   MOBILE PHONE BEING DROPPED INSIDE SUIT OF ARMOUR

*SAV:*   *Ouch! What, who's there?*

*F/X:*   CLANKING ARMOUR

*JOYCE:*   *Shall I hold the helmet while you get out?*

*F/X:*   CLANKING ARMOUR

*SAV:*   *I was, um, just checking it for rust, Joyce.*

You can see that the same story is told in different ways depending on the medium.

## Writing for performance

Writing for performance is about more than just the words. The performers will add to the comedy at many levels – just the way someone looks, their hair and clothes, will have an effect on the audience. The performer's body language creates another level, and physical comedy is an art form in its own right. Performers add timing, rhythm and, in live media, sensitivity to the audience to your script.

Inevitably this means that the performance will be different from the pictures you saw in your head as you were writing. It also means that the more you understand about performance, the more accurate those pictures are likely to be. The best way to gain that understanding is to try it yourself, for instance at a local open mic night or in an amateur dramatic group.

Apart from radio (see later), performance is intensely visual and scripts need to reflect that. Characters reveal themselves through their actions as much as their words.

**Comedy insight – COUNT ARTHUR STRONG**
*Although everything should, of course, be a collaboration, amazingly the writer's contribution is often overlooked or undervalued, never forget, without them there are no words to say. Try that hat on for size, all you actors and directors.*

Count Arthur Strong, via Steve Delaney

## Recorded performance

Apart from radio, costs are high in recorded media. Bear this in mind when you're deciding about outside filming, special effects and so on. More than anywhere else the writer is part of a team, and the director (or in radio the producer) will have as much or even more creative input. The piece is created at the editing stage rather than at the writing stage.

It's important to gain an understanding of the role of the camera in TV and movies. It moves, taking the viewer with it. It creates point of view (usually abbreviated to pov) so that the viewer can see events from the perspective of more than one character. It also allows for close-ups, taking the viewer right into the characters' emotions and responses.

### TELEVISION

Television comedy is the most easily accessible for most of us, and so it tends to set the benchmark. It's so easy to change channels that it's important to grab the attention of the audience immediately, and keep their interest going.

Sometimes there is a studio audience to give a live feel that helps the actors, but where there is no studio audience the performers may need a fuller script to help them find their rhythm. Rehearsal time is short for TV, so performers need to get into the script and find the laughs immediately. TV performances are small and intimate.

**For more on this see *Write A Play And Get It Performed* which has a chapter on TV.**

### MOVIES

In the UK movies are low budget, since the market is so much smaller than in the US, and so comedy has to come from the interactions between characters rather than expensive location filming or special effects – *Shaun of the Dead* is a good example.

Movie audiences are less likely to be distracted than those watching TV at home, and in fact they will need time to settle into their seats and get focused – this is the job of the opening credits and the first few moments of the action. Since the audience can't change channels, and they've paid for their seats, they will usually be willing to give the movie a chance. Once a movie goes to DVD of course it will be watched in the home like TV.

Plots usually have to be constructed in great detail using a technique known as storyboarding. This is rather like drawing out the plot in cartoon form. The director has pretty well total control of a movie, and both in the shooting and the editing processes the original script can be changed beyond recognition.

**For more on this see *Break into Screenwriting*.**

### RADIO

Radio is a unique medium and in the UK the BBC has a long history of delivering all kinds of comedy on radio. Radio audiences are loyal but are often listening at home, while getting on with other tasks, or in the car. Catch their interest from the opening moments or they'll be likely to change stations or switch off.

Scriptwriters have virtually limitless freedom in their choice of locations, sound effects and music. You can have as many sets as you want, furnished with no regard to budget. You can be in Cleopatra's Palace one moment and on the moon the next.

On the other hand there is the discipline of conveying everything with sound, predominantly dialogue. Dialogue has to reveal character, move the plot forward, convey information and, of course, create laughs. Don't bring on characters in groups, allow time for the listener to get used to each new voice. Find ways to repeat the characters' names from time to time.

Sound effects and background sounds help with these tasks of course. We learn something if a character shuts a door with a quiet click, or slams it. The plot is moved forward if the sound of a car's engine is interrupted by the sound of the car crashing. Information comes from background noises such as an owl hooting or waves crashing on a seashore. All of these can convey laughs if used in the right way.

We can also of course hear the character's thoughts, as long as the listener is always quite clear that it's the inner voice they're hearing. Music can also be used to create laughs, usually by being quite inappropriate for the scene.

**For more on this see *Write A Play And Get It Performed* which has a chapter on radio.**

---

## Live performance

Live performance has to be bigger and broader than performance for a camera. Don't make the mistake of assuming an audience can see small movements and subtle facial expressions. The interaction between performers and audience means that no two nights will ever be the same, and your script will have good days and bad days.

### THEATRE

Like a cinema audience, theatre audiences need a little time to settle down but are then likely to give the play, sketch show or stand-up their full attention.

There is a longer rehearsal period for theatre than for movies or TV, and also plays are often given an out-of-town tryout with the specific aim of fine-tuning the script. This doesn't mean you can send in a rough draft. Always send your best work, but accept the opportunity to polish it even further.

For more on this see *Write A Play And Get It Performed.*

### COMEDY CLUBS

Comedy clubs are where most stand-up comics start their careers and they provide quite a different environment and different audience to a theatre or concert hall. The entertainment is just one part of the whole experience, which includes drinks and socializing. So the audience is likely to be more restless, with people constantly going to the bar or the toilets, and less focused, since they are likely to interact with the people around them.

Alcohol loosens the tongue as we all know so heckling is likely to be more frequent and possibly more aggressive. As the writer you can only do a certain amount to protect the performer from all this, but a strong funny script and a few heckle responses worked out in advance will give them a good start.

For more on this see *Be A Great Stand-up.*

# Print

In contrast to performance, experiencing print media is usually a solitary experience. Words and images on a page or screen give the writer a direct line to the reader's mind. A reader can look back and read again if they get confused about a plot or just don't get a joke. Equally they can dip in and out as they feel like it.

### JOURNALISM

Humorous journalism is usually in the form of a regular weekly or monthly column. Pieces are short, between 500 and 1,000 words. Rather like a sketch, a short humorous piece will usually have a single connecting thread that leads the reader to a surprise ending. An eye-catching title is the best way to persuade readers to stop at the column and read it.

For more on this see *Get Your Articles Published.*

Someone picking up a novel has chosen to spend some time reading and brings a certain amount of willingness to engage with the story – although they will soon put the book down if they aren't enjoying it. The plot can develop as quickly or as slowly as you choose, but there must be something on every page to keep the reader interested.

**For more on this see *Write A Novel And Get It Published*.**

---

## Internet

Initially Internet reading seemed to be about finding a website by chance, looking quickly round and then moving on, but gradually readers have started to develop loyalties and will return to their favourites.

Understanding how to write for the Internet in still in its infancy. It's become clear that readers prefer to click rather than scroll, so think in terms of enough words to fill one screen. Internet readers have very short attention spans so you need to get their attention immediately. Short paragraphs and short sentences are much easier to cope with on-screen.

A blog is a good way to get your humour out there. Don't waffle, or use the blog for different purposes – if you build up a following for your wacky comedy then don't suddenly start blogging about the cute things your toddler said, or the irritation you feel about traffic jams.

### Exercise

Take something you've already written and rewrite it for a different medium.

# Things to remember

▶ There is crossover between various media.

▶ Performance is a team effort.

▶ TV and radio audiences are easily distracted.

▶ Movie and theatre audiences are more focused.

▶ Reading is a solitary activity.

▶ Keep Internet writing short.

# 18

······································································

# Other types of comedy writing

In this chapter you will learn:
- *about drawn comedy*
- *about poetry and songwriting*
- *about other markets for comedy.*

*Note: This chapter gives some brief guidelines about other types of comedy writing and refers you to other books in the Teach Yourself series that go into greater detail.*

This book has focused very much on writing for performance and writing prose, but there are many other ways to write comedy. Some are simply other outlets for existing work, others are highly specialized forms of writing. However the basics of comedy writing apply throughout – a joke's a joke, it's how you tell it that varies.

### ANIMATION

This is a specialized and complex art form. It includes drawn animation (such as *The Simpsons*), model animation (*Wallace and Gromit*), cut-out animation (*South Park*) and computer animation (*Toy Story*). Computer Generated Imagery (CGI) has created a form that includes both real and animated (*The Mask, Who Framed Roger Rabbit?*). Clearly the laws of physics don't apply in animation and characters can be made to do the impossible. Writers have to think visually and characters need to be very strongly defined. Audiences seem to find it easier to engage with very extreme satirical material in animation, perhaps because it is at several removes from reality.

## CARTOONS

Animated movies are often called cartoons, but here we're looking at strips and single-frame cartoons that you might find in a newspaper or magazine. Surprisingly, you don't need to be able to draw beautifully. You can either devise your own rough and ready style or work with an artist.

**Comedy insight – PAUL HAYES-WATKINS**

*Many of the contributions come into the magazine digitally now, which is perfectly acceptable. However, I would request that once the cartoonist has scanned and prepared their work for despatch... please, please, please don't feel the need to colour the cartoons with the airbrush colouring tool! If the cartoon really needs colour – put it on the traditional way.*

Paul Hayes-Watkins is the Art director of *Saga* magazine

Remember that we read English from top to bottom and left to right. The drawing part of a cartoon is almost always the equivalent of the set-up to a joke and the text, which is along the bottom, is the punchline. Speech bubbles however are usually towards the top, so the reader will absorb them at the same time as they take in the content of the drawing. Have as few words as possible in a frame – 25 is the maximum.

**Comedy insight – KEV F SUTHERLAND**

*In comics, many first-time writers forget there are pictures and don't use them. Talking heads make for very boring comics, and too many words run the risk of it stopping being a comic strip at all. (Some comics writers put in so many words it becomes clear they actually want to write stuff that's not comics.)*

Kev F Sutherland is a comedian and comic artist (*Beano, Marvel, Viz*, etc.)

Three or four frame cartoons are rather like quickies. If you're creating a series, you'll need sustainable ideas – some cartoons run for decades. There is no character development in that type of cartoon, and the focus is always on the main character – Garfield for instance. The first frame contains the set-up, the next two or three frames develop it and the final frame contains the punchline. Again be extremely economical with words, dialogue needs to be as short as possible and any captions must be to the point.

### CHILDREN

Children love to laugh and acquire an instinctive understanding of comedy at an early age. Younger children like silly slapstick humour, older children enjoy joke books but also demand satisfying stories. Avoid sentimentality, satire, sarcasm and irony. Tell the story from the child's point of view. Children like to see the adult world undermined in some way, and they like a strong moral code with the good guys winning in the end.

For more on this see *Write a Children's Book And Get it Published*.

### GREETINGS CARDS AND E-CARDS

The market for humorous greetings cards is huge and once again you don't have to be able to draw, as companies will buy your ideas and add the artwork (of course you can expect to earn more if you can also supply the artwork). A humorous card is basically a joke – the front of the card, both words and pictures, is the set-up and the inside of the card is the punchline. It's important to keep cards personal, so use 'I', 'Me' and 'You'.

### PANTOMIME

The world of professional pantomime writing can be extremely difficult to break into, but there is a strong market for scripts for amateur groups. Of course a panto is not a pure comedy and the comedy elements are usually confined to two or three characters. It's a writing challenge as you'll need to include something for the children as well as something for the adults that the children won't understand. As well as jokes arising out of character and plot you'll need to tack on slapstick and topical jokes.

For more on this see *Write a Play And Get It Performed*, which has a chapter on panto.

### POETRY

There is a strong humorous element to the current poetry scene, and this is particularly true of performance poetry. However the whole point of it is that the poet performs their own work. There are also numerous print outlets for poetry, although very few of them are able to pay.

For more on this see *Write Poetry And Get It Published* which has a short chapter on performance poetry.

### RADIO DJs

There are so many radio stations and each DJ needs material – they have to say something in between the music tracks and there's a particular need for amusing chat on the breakfast time and drive time shows, when commuters are listening on car radios.

### SONGWRITING

Comic songwriting is a specialized discipline, but there is always a demand, especially on news-based radio shows like *The Now Show*, where Mitch Benn contributes songs on topical subjects. More often than not the writer is also the performer. There's also a strong crossover between comedy and music – see performers like Bill Bailey, *The Flight of the Conchords* and *The Mighty Boosh*.

If you use existing tunes you need to be aware of copyright issues.

For more on this see *Get Started in Songwriting*.

### TRAINING AND SPEECHWRITING

Training and speechwriting are two more specialized disciplines that can be interesting and lucrative. Both make use of humour to keep the attention of the listeners and to make hard information more easily absorbed. Politicians often employ separate gag writers to inject some comedy into the material produced by their speech-writers.

Don't expect your clients to have the same skills as professional performers – you'll need to write material that is easy for them to put across. Meet them if possible, so that you get a feel for how they talk naturally and do everything you can to persuade them to rehearse.

For more on this see *The Clinton Factor: Communicating with Charisma*.

### T-SHIRTS, BUMPER STICKERS, MUGS AND SO ON

All of these and more use jokes and manufacturers will pay for them.

# Things to remember

▶ Animation can break taboos.

▶ Cartoons need very few words.

▶ Children love to laugh.

▶ There are many outlets for comedy.

# 19

Practicalities of placing your work

In this chapter you will learn:
- *about working for free*
- *about submissions*
- *how to advance your career.*

---

**Comedy insight – TONY STAVEACRE**

*The most common mistake that new comedy writers make is to try to get inside the mind of the commissioning editor on whose opinion the future of a project will depend. This is impossible. Anyway, you really don't want to go there. Look at the sequence of rejection slips that all great classic comedy ideas have collected before they hit the mark. P. G. Wodehouse papered the walls of his bedroom with rejection slips. Accept the grim fact that most commissioning editors are idiots who have no sense of humour. Make it your plan to find the one salaried suit who is on your wavelength. That will take a bit of determined research.*

Tony Staveacre is a writer/producer in TV, radio and theatre

---

People write for all sorts of reasons – fame, fortune, therapy and compulsion. Some people know from the very beginning that they are aiming for an audience, others realize later on that they need to get their work out there. I suspect that very few writers are completely satisfied with the process of writing and are content if no one else ever sees their work. Of course there's no real way of knowing, since by definition they are unknown to the wider world. However on the assumption that you would like to reach an audience, here are a few tips on how to go about it.

## Working for free

There are many opportunities for a writer to work for nothing. From the smallest village magazine to a theatre company with no budget to pay a writer, you will find plenty of outlets.

They can provide a reasonable training ground, although some are more useful to an ambitious writer than others. Your local badminton club may be so desperate for someone to write the newsletter that you'll never get any helpful feedback on your attempts to lighten it with some comedy, whereas your local amateur dramatic group will almost certainly go the other extreme and be very cautious about putting on a production by an unknown writer. (In case you were wondering, this is because they usually need to fill the seats to keep the books balanced, and an Alan Ayckbourn play is more likely to do that than yours.)

At the start of your career it's worth taking up some of these opportunities, but try to see them as a stepping stone not a stopping place.

## Submissions – common ground

Whether you want to place a sitcom or a novel, there are certain things that are common to all submission processes. At the start of your career most of your submissions will be cold calling, where you send work out to people and organizations that haven't asked to see it. You have to persuade them that you are talented, reliable and worth investing in. Luckily, everyone is looking for the next big thing, so there will always be a way in for new writers. It isn't easy though, so do everything you can to improve the odds in your favour. Remember your day job keeps you in touch with the real world and use that to your advantage.

In some cases you'll need to send a proposal (for a drama) or a treatment (for a movie) or a synopsis (for a novel) rather than the finished work. In all these cases create something straightforward that explains the proposed work in simple terms. Don't strain to be funny, and don't keep any secrets – even if the piece has a surprise ending, it's only meant to be a surprise for the audience. Demonstrate the quality of your comedy writing by enclosing sample pages from the proposed work. These should be fully polished, not a draft, and give a real flavour of what you're suggesting. Always send your best work.

Exercise

**Write a synopsis for a piece of your own writing.**

EXERCISE

Always do some research into the organization concerned before you submit. Most of this can be done online, and also there are directories like *The Writers' and Artists' Yearbook* and *The Writers' Handbook*. There's no point in submitting a comic novel to a publisher that only publishes romance. At best you'll have wasted your time and at worst you'll have created a bad impression that might just have a knock-on effect. Many organizations have writers' guidelines – check these and be sure to conform to them.

Make your submission as professional-looking as possible. Spellcheck your work, then read it through to double-check for mistakes. Lay it out cleanly. Check whether the organization concerned prefers electronic or paper submissions.

If you're posting hard copy, never send handwritten work and always keep a copy or computer back-up. Print it out on one side of white A4 paper in black ink. Use a simple font (Arial, Times New Roman or Courier) and 12 point size. Leave wide margins at the top, bottom and sides to allow readers room to make notes. Number the pages and fasten together in the top left hand corner – many readers like to take the fastener out and read loose pages, so make it easy for them. The numbering means they can be re-assembled easily if dropped. Include your contact details on the first page.

Don't add anything in the way of photos and drawings and don't have it professionally bound – these are the marks of an amateur.

Devise a simple system for record keeping, so that you know where a piece of work has been sent, on what date and what the result was.

### COVERING LETTER

Include a covering letter (or email). Keep it short – one page is enough. Never start it 'Dear Sir or Madam'. Find out the name of the relevant person, by checking the website or phoning. Keep the letter simple and to the point, and don't try to be funny. You only need three paragraphs:

1 Say who you are and describe briefly the work you are submitting, or the idea you are proposing.
2 Say briefly why you think your work will be of interest to the audience and what makes it different.
3 Say something about yourself that gives the impression you are both professional and talented.

### YOUR CV

Include a CV if you think it's appropriate. Keep it to one page and be sure to include your contact details. Only include personal information if it's relevant to the work concerned. The same applies to your education, hobbies and jobs. Most of the page should be about your writing life. If you're at the start of your career you might feel there isn't much to say, but include everything you've done. Even if you can't claim anything impressive, it will still show that you take writing seriously and spend time doing it rather than dreaming about doing it. Present yourself in the best possible light (no self-deprecating jokes) but don't on any account tell lies – you'll be found out for sure.

> **Author insight**
> I knew someone who mentioned 'fluent French' on their CV. At the interview they were asked a question in French, couldn't answer it, and didn't get the job.

Keep the CV short and to the point. Don't use fancy fonts, gimmicky layouts or artwork in the hope of getting noticed – let your writing do that for you.

### FEEDBACK AND REJECTION

It can take a long time before you get a response. Don't make a nuisance of yourself by asking what's happening to your work.

Start writing something else, and if you haven't heard anything in six weeks then send an enquiry.

If you're very lucky you'll get some feedback when the submission is returned to you. At one time organizations routinely employed readers to write short reports on unsolicited submissions, but that is fairly rare now. Some writing competitions include feedback on entries which can be useful.

However the feedback reaches you, you'll need to develop a tough skin and keep an open mind. The tough skin is because some feedback is very cruel. You need the open mind because it's very easy to leap immediately to the defence of your precious work. Try to understand what the feedback is saying, and whether, just possibly, it could be right. Of course the reader is only one person; you'll know nothing about who they are and whether they have any experience and insight, and you have to bear that in mind too.

## Comedy insight – SUE LIMB

*The most common mistake that new comedy writers make is being prickly and possessive about a piece of work and hypersensitive to criticism. Sometimes you just have to throw stuff out and start again.*

Sue Limb is a comedy writer (Dulcie Domum, *Up the Garden Path*, *The Wordsmiths at Gorsemere*)

In most instances all you're going to get is a simple rejection, and you're going to have to learn to deal with it. (Dealing with success can be hard too, but hopefully if it happens to you, you'll be able to afford an expensive therapist.)

If someone is interested in your work you may well be invited in for discussions – as a result of which you may be asked to write something entirely different. You may also be asked to sign a release form before any meeting or discussion. This will acknowledge that the ideas behind your work may not be unique and that the organization may well be considering other, similar ideas. You may not like doing this, but you'll have no choice. You will still own the copyright in your words, but there is no copyright in ideas.

# Submissions – specifics

## JOKES, CARTOONS AND GREETINGS CARDS

Always submit jokes in batches – at least ten at a time. Twenty would be better. The only exception to this is if the BBC has a programme with an open submissions policy, where they will look at everything, even a single joke. At the time of writing, *Newsjack* on Radio 7 was the only open door programme (see Taking it further).

Stand-up comedians often write their own material at first, but as they become more successful they sometimes need more material than they can generate. Use the Internet to find the name of their agent and make contact that way.

Similarly with submitting cartoons, send several to show you have staying power. Number each frame and include an explanation of visuals if you are sending sketches for another artist to draw.

With greetings cards, check the writers' guidelines for each company and be prepared to send several ideas at a time.

## SKETCHES

Again, submit in batches, although don't overwhelm the reader – send between four and six sketches at a time. Give each sketch a title so that it can be easily identified and use the appropriate script layout.

### SCRIPTS

For all types of script make clear distinctions between speeches and instructions such as stage directions. Don't allow speeches to run across two pages and put END at the end of the script.

#### MOVIE, TV AND RADIO

Movie, TV and radio all have standard formats for laying out a script. The BBC standard layouts can be downloaded from their website (see Taking it further).

If you're sending a proposal it should summarize the premise in a few words. Go on to say what is special about it, and in particular what will appeal to the audience. Then expand on the idea, giving detail, and provide the answers to any obvious practical and budgetary questions.

If you want to write for radio DJs, start by contacting your local station and offering them your services.

#### THEATRE

There is no accepted standard layout for theatre scripts but do make sure your layout is simple and easily understood. Here are a few layout guidelines that most readers will be happy with:

▶ Create a title page with the name of the play, your name and your contact details.
▶ Create brief descriptions of characters, the set and props.
▶ Distinguish between speeches and everything else such as the speaker's name and stage directions. Using capitals for everything except speeches is the easiest way to do this.
▶ Keep the speakers' names on the left hand side of the page. Some readers like to cover the names and read the speeches alone to see if they can tell who is speaking (if they can't, it's a black mark).
▶ Have single line spacing within speeches and double line spacing between speeches, and between speeches and stage directions.
▶ If a direction falls within a speech, put it in brackets as well as in capitals.

#### JOURNALISM

Most publications have their own writers' guidelines, and these are often on the website. You should submit either a proposal or a fully finished piece – never send a draft or notes. While most editors prefer proposals, in the case of comedy they do need to see a sample of your work. Always include a word count.

### PUBLISHING

Most publishers have submissions guidelines on their websites. As a basic rule send a synopsis (500 words maximum) and three sample chapters for a novel.

### THE INTERNET

There are plenty of websites specifically for writers, and other websites that need written material. Some of these are looking for comedy but very few of them pay. Be sure you understand what you're getting into, in other words, read the small print. Once your work is on the web it's very easily stolen, and even though you own the copyright it can be virtually impossible to keep control of it.

---

## Other factors

### AGENTS

For some types of writing it's possible to work through an agent who will help place work, negotiate fees and so on, in return for a percentage of your earnings. At the beginning of your career, when you most need an agent, it will be difficult to persuade one to take you on, whereas once you're successful it'll be much easier. If you decide to look for an agent, approach them in exactly the same way as any other submission.

### COPYRIGHT

*Please note copyright law is complicated and these notes are not comprehensive*

You automatically own the copyright in everything you write and you don't need to register your copyright, although if you suspect your work has been stolen you might need to prove when you wrote it. If you work on a computer then that is taken care of by the way documents are dated. However there is no copyright in ideas, and you'll inevitably find that other writers have had similar ideas to you. In practice most organizations are honourable and it is very rare to have your copyright abused.

### FOREIGN MARKETS

Those of us who write in English are lucky. Not only is there a large English-speaking community out there, but many countries have English as their second language. Holland and Germany have a long tradition of buying material from English comedy writers. Buyers there and in other countries are happy to arrange translation. Clearly you need to remove all wordplay jokes, and all but the most basic of English idioms. It goes without saying that visual comedy sells well in foreign markets.

### NETWORKING

There are endless opportunities for networking. Unless you live somewhere extraordinarily remote, start with your local community. Join any writers' groups, or maybe start one. Attend workshops and courses, as much for the people you'll meet as anything else. If you're interested in playwriting visit your local theatre regularly and check if they have any writers' schemes. If journalism is your thing, ask the editor of your local paper if they'll take some humorous pieces. You simply never know where these things might lead.

Then there's the Internet. You can join any number of forums and networking sites. Don't let them take over your life, but do try to have a presence. If you can set up your own website, then do so, then you can build up traffic by always including a link to it in everything you do.

### SHOWREELS

Where there is a performance element to your writing you may want to send a showreel, either of yourself or of someone performing your work. You can pay to have a professional showreel made, but it is possible to create your own. It is meant to be a sample so keep it to five minutes or under. Just like any other submission it should be immaculately presented with your contact details included.

## Things to remember

▶ Use working for free as a training opportunity.

▶ Always submit your best work, immaculately presented.

▶ Research organizations before you submit.

▶ Feedback can hurt, but often contains something useful.

▶ Use clear simple layouts.

▶ Check writers' guidelines.

# 20

## Doing it yourself

In this chapter you will learn:
- *how to get your work before an audience*
- *about the work involved*
- *that you can't expect to cover costs.*

Note: *This chapter gives some brief guidelines and refers you to other books in the Teach Yourself series that go into greater detail.*

If your work has been rejected, and you have faith in it, then you could think of going it alone. Rejection can be for all sorts of reasons apart from poor quality. Organizations have limited budgets for a start, or they might already have committed to something that is too similar to your work.

---

**Comedy insight – KEN ROCK**
*Don't give up. If your script is rejected it doesn't mean it's no good. It's just not right for that person.*

Ken Rock is President of the British Society of Comedy Writers

---

## DIY – common ground

The main advantage of getting your work in front of an audience is the simple pleasure it will give you. It's immensely fulfilling to hear a group of people laughing at your jokes, or to have someone say how much they enjoyed your novel.

Then there's the business of feedback. You can get this in various ways – from the audience, from reviews, from anyone involved in the production process. You can seek it out, for instance by including a questionnaire in a theatre programme, or an email address in a book. However it arrives, take note of it and use it to improve your writing. In fact, always do a rewrite where possible – after a performance for instance. It's not possible to rewrite a novel once it's published, but you can learn lessons for the next one.

You can use your DIY comedy project as a marketing tool for your future career. Make sure it reaches the industry professionals – send them free tickets, or free copies of books and recordings. If it is successful, then you can use it as a stepping stone into the industry.

Of course there are difficulties. The main one is that it will be a lot of work, and most of that work isn't writing. Instead of writing comedy, the one thing you really want to do, you'll be getting your head round print runs, or actors' insurance, or how the camcorder works. This all takes time and energy, both of which you'd probably rather devote to writing.

### FINANCES

Another big difficulty is cost. You'll have to pay all the costs upfront with no guarantee of getting your money back. In fact you're almost certain to make a loss, so it's best to write that money off from the start. Always establish what the costs will be before you commit yourself to the project. Make a list of everything you'll need to pay for, and add a contingency fund.

### MARKETING

Most of us don't have the skills or resources for publicity and marketing, and yet these are absolutely vital to any DIY effort. You can't build a career on the sales you make to your friends and family.

For most, DIY marketing is the biggest difficulty. Unless you already have fantastic contacts in the media it is going to be hard work. Write a sparkling press release and send it to all your local publications, and any national ones that you think might be interested. Also send it to local TV and radio stations. Include a review copy if your work is a book, and free tickets if it's a performance. Offer to talk about your work to local clubs, and take along copies or tickets to sell. Think laterally, and do whatever you can to push your work in front of the public.

# DIY – specifics

## STAND-UP ROUTINES

If you're an eccentric millionaire then by all means start your own comedy club. Otherwise, the DIY route with jokes is to get involved with your local open mic night, either at a club or a pub. If you are really determined not to perform them yourself, then you'll need a friend who has performing ambitions, or who at the very least enjoys performing.

The normal set for these nights is three to five minutes – check with the venue. In fact visit the venue as an audience member first. Familiarize yourself with the set-up and get to know the staff if possible.

Whoever is performing, be sure to rehearse the act, and try it out in front of a few willing victims beforehand. On the night, arrive early and remind yourself that the audience is there to enjoy themselves – they'll want to meet you halfway. However well it's going, a comic should get off in good time; it's always best to leave them wanting more. Make friends with the other performers, be supportive to them rather than critical – they may want to buy your material one day.

For more about stand-up, see *Be A Great Stand-up*.

## GREETINGS CARDS

If you find it easy to write jokey greetings for special occasions then it's comparatively easy to start a small card business. Obviously you'll need access to good artwork that captures the mood of the moment. Research what's around by browsing in your local card shop. You'll need to find a competent printer, as not all of them can manage high-quality colour printing. The easiest way to market cards is to ask local shops to take a few on a sale or return basis, but you could also take a stall at local markets or go to car boot sales.

## THEATRE

You can put on a production of your own play, or a review if you want to showcase your sketches. Start by deciding who is going to direct, because they'll choose the actors. Finding the people you need is where networking really comes in useful. Use all your contacts to find resting professionals, or talented amateurs. Drama students are often interested in gaining experience on small projects, so make contact with local educational establishments. They may also be able to help you find a lighting person, sound person, and set and costume designers. You'll need a backstage crew, front of house, and people to help with setting up and clearing out. That adds up to quite a few people. If you struggle to find people willing to put effort into your play or review, then perhaps it isn't good enough yet and needs a rewrite.

Once you've got the people in place, there's still more to do. You'll need a venue – there are plenty of small halls and pub theatres to choose from. You'll also need a separate rehearsal space – your living room won't be big enough. Don't forget insurance. Check what insurance the venue has and top it up if necessary.

You'll need to create programmes and tickets – use the programme as a publicity opportunity for everyone involved. Include a number and email address for Box Office – it's unlikely the venue will do this so you'll probably end up selling the tickets yourself. Use the artwork from the programme to create flyers which you can spread around the local area to publicize the performances.

It's worth videoing a performance to help you with the inevitable rewrite. The quality won't be good enough to send out professionally, but it will mean you have a record.

For more on this see *Write a Play And Get It Performed* or *Make Your Show a Success*.

> ### Author insight
>
> When Ann Gawthorpe and I put on a small professional production of our play *Over Exposure* we both worked on it full time for three months. It really does need that many hours of input to do it properly.

### TV AND RADIO

No, unfortunately, you can't just start up your own TV or radio station (yes, I know there are pirate stations out there, but you're on your own with that one). You can however record your work and send it out to production companies, or post it on the Internet. You'll need the appropriate equipment and a reasonable level of technical competence. You can perform your own work if it is a solo effort, otherwise go through the process of finding a director, actors and a crew.

## MOVIES

There is no legal reason why you shouldn't set up your own independent movie company (known as an Indie) but the most likely way to showcase your work for film is to make a short and enter it for competitions. You'll need a cast and crew for anything other than a video of you doing stand-up, so just like with theatre you'll need to network, and track down students of film making.

**For more on this see *Get Started in Film Making*.**

### JOURNALISM AND CARTOONS

If you can't find an outlet for your humorous journalism and cartoons, then consider starting your own magazine or comic. Magazines for adults generally rely on advertising to achieve financial balance and somebody has to sell the space – this involves a lot of cold calling and salesmanship. You'll also need to have the magazines printed, as home printers are not up to the job, and a means of distribution.

You'll need to keep up a steady flow of material, unless you offer space to other comedy writers. Cartoons of course will need drawing, so if you're only good at the words you'll need to buddy up with an artist.

**For more on this see *Get Your Articles Published* which has a chapter on starting your own magazine.**

### SELF-PUBLISHING A NOVEL OR JOKE BOOK

It's perfectly possible to publish your own comedy book. There are plenty of small printers and bookbinders who will produce the book for you. You'll need a cover design, something eye-catching and stylish, and there will be decisions to make about font, page layout and margins. You'll be responsible for editing and proofreading, but both these tasks are best carried out by someone else, who comes to the book fresh. You'll need somewhere to store the copies and above all you'll need to market the book.

If you are hoping to place the book in bookshops it will need an International Standard Book Number, and this will also enable you to sell it on Amazon through their Advantage scheme.

There are companies that will publish your book for you, for a fee of course. It's very important to distinguish between companies that genuinely help you publish and those that offer what is known as vanity publishing, where you pay a lot of money for a few fancy copies of your book.

You can also use Internet tools, such as CreateSpace and Lulu to publish a book.

There is more on this in *Get Your Book Published*.

### INTERNET

Most forms of writing can be posted on the Internet. You can write for a blog, or twitter, or on your own website. You can upload songs and videos onto YouTube, metacafe or one of the many alternatives. As long as you've got Internet access the cost is minimal – the real challenge is to build a following. The American comedian Bo Burnham started his career on YouTube, so it can be done.

---

# Edinburgh Fringe

The Edinburgh Fringe is hugely important to the world of comedy. The publicity tends to focus on stand-up performers and the competition to win the annual award for stand-up, but there is a lot more to it than that.

The first key thing to understand about the Edinburgh Fringe is that anyone can take a show there. Most festivals have a creative director who chooses who will appear, but for three weeks in August anyone can make their mark in Edinburgh as long as they can find enough money to pay for a venue. The second key thing is that vast numbers of powerful people in the world of entertainment, most of whom are London-based, decamp to Edinburgh for the Festival. It is the one place where dreams might come true, and there really might be someone in the audience for your show who can change your life.

Of course it is heavily performance-oriented, and writers have to either turn themselves into performers or find people who will make their work come alive.

The best way to go about this is to spend a few days at the Festival one summer, with a view to taking a show there the following summer. You'll get a feel for the smaller venues, which are the only ones most of us can afford. You'll see what hard work it is, and learn from other people's mistakes. Then you'll have a whole year to organize your show, and believe me you'll need it.

## Things to remember

▶ You can learn a lot from direct contact with your audience.

▶ You can choose to perform your own stand-up routine.

▶ Putting on a play is a huge undertaking, but possible.

▶ TV and film are very costly and technically demanding.

▶ Magazines require a constant flow of material.

▶ It's easy to publish a novel, but hard to market it.

▶ It costs nothing to post on the Internet.

▶ The Edinburgh Fringe is an open door for new talent.

# Taking it further

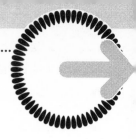

## Books

### COMEDY WRITING

Ashton, Brad, *How to Write Comedy* (Hamish Hamilton, 1983).

Byrne, John, *Writing Comedy* (A&C Black, 3rd edn., 2005).

Byrne, John and Powell, Marcus, *Writing Sitcoms* (A&C Black, 2003).

Helitzer, Mel with Shatz, Mark, *Comedy Writing Secrets* (Writer's Digest Books, 2005). Highly recommended, although aimed at the American market.

Perret, Gene, *Comedy Writing Step by Step* (Quill Driver Books, revised edn., 2007). Highly recommended, although aimed at the American market.

Wolfe, Ronald, *Writing Comedy* (Robert Hale, revised edn., 2003).

### GENERAL

*The Oxford Manual Of Style* (Oxford University Press).

*The Writers' Handbook* (Pan McMillan).

*Writers' and Artists' Yearbook* (A&C Black).

Fieldhouse, Harry, *Everyman's Good English Guide* (J. M. Dent, 1982).

Gowers, Ernest, Greenbaum, Sidney and Whitcut, Janet, *The Complete Plain Words* (HMSO, 2004).

Partridge, Eric, *Usage and Abusage* (Book Club Associates, 1980).

Room, Adrian, *Dictionary of Confusibles* (Routledge & Kegan Paul, 1979).

# DVD

Rowan Atkinson's excellent series on comedy, known as both *Funny Business* and *Laughing Matters* is available on DVD but can be hard to track down.

# Courses

### JAN ETHERINGTON'S COMEDY WRITING COURSE

Award-winning comedy writer, Jan Etherington holds two-day comedy writing courses at Riverside Arts Centre, in Sunbury on Thames, Middlesex.

Jan co-created the prime-time hit television comedy series, *Second Thoughts, Faith In The Future, Next of Kin* and *Duck Patrol* plus many radio comedies and is also a successful journalist and broadcaster.

More detail www.comedycourse.biz

Tel: 07887 907713

Or email: comedycourse@hotmail.co.uk

### MINDY GLAZER'S SITCOM WRITING COURSE

Mindy Glazer currently teaches sitcom writing on ed2go.com, the largest purveyor of online classes in the English-speaking world. She wrote for *Who's the Boss, Kate and Allie,* and *My Two Dads,* among other shows. She is also the author of three novels, non-fiction, magazine and newspaper pieces. Her class, Breaking Into Sitcom Writing, was among the first college-level sitcom writing classes.

www.ed2go.com then search for 'sitcom writing'

### ARVON

Short residential courses including specific comedy writing courses www.arvonfoundation.org.

### NATIONAL WRITERS' CENTRE FOR WALES

Week-long residential writing courses, not specifically about comedy.
www.tynewydd.org

### SWANWICK SUMMER SCHOOL

Week-long residential courses in Swanwick near Derby, check
programme for comedy.
www.wss.org.uk

### BA (HONS) COMEDY – WRITING AND PERFORMANCE (FULL TIME)

Southampton Solent University
East Park Terrace
Southampton
Hampshire
SO14 0YN
Telephone: +44 (0)23 8031 9000

Facsimile: +44 (0)23 8022 2259

Email: ask@solent.ac.uk

www.solent.ac.uk

### INTRODUCTION TO COMEDY WRITING

Richmond Adult Community College
Parkshot
Richmond
London
TW9 2RE

General enquiries: 020 8891 5907

Email: Info:racc.ac.uk

www.racc.ac.uk

---

## Magazines

*Writers' Forum*, monthly. www.writers-forum.com

*Writing Magazine*, monthly. Subscribers also receive *Writers' News*.
www.writersnews.co.uk

# Organizations

**Society of Authors** www.societyofauthors.net

**British Society of Comedy Writers** www.bscw.co.uk/what_is.htm

**The Writers' Guild of Great Britain** www.writersguild.org.uk

**The Authors' Licensing and Collecting Society** is able to remunerate authors with secondary royalties via collective licensing schemes from photocopying etc. www.alcs.co.uk

**Public Lending Right** is administered by Public Lending Right based in Stockton-upon-Tees and funded by the Department of Culture, Media and Sport (DCMS). www.plr.uk.com

**Funny Women**

Through Funny Women we actively encourage all aspects of female comedy and recognize that writing is as important as performing. Our workshops encourage writing skills as much as performance and we are introducing a Comic Writing Award into the Funny Women Awards this year. We will partner aspiring writers with performers who have a genuine need to collaborate on material. We also coach performers on how to develop their material and the icing on the cake is our platform for performance where it all comes together – through the Funny Women Awards, our annual new talent competition, and our regular showcases around the UK.

Lynne Parker – Producer
Funny Women Ltd.
St. David's House
15 Worple Way
Richmond-upon-Thames
London
TW10 6DG

Office: 020 8948 4444 Mobile: 07973 470577

www.funnywomen.com

### The Greeting Card Association

The Greeting Card Association has lots of information on writing for greeting cards, including a list of publishers looking for freelance writers, in the Resources section of its website. See: www.greetingcardassociation.org.uk

---

## Websites

### SELF-PUBLISHING

Two websites where you can self-publish at no cost, or pay a small amount for extra services:

**CreateSpace** www.createspace.com

**Lulu** www.lulu.com

### THE BRITISH COMEDY GUIDE

Comprehensive website including help and information for comedy writers. www.comedy.co.uk

### WRITER'S DIGEST

An American site for all types of writing. www.writersdigest.com

### ROYAL TELEVISION SOCIETY

Useful advice on writing for television. www.rts.org.uk

### THE WRITER'S ROOM AT THE BBC

For all information on writing for the BBC. www.bbc.co.uk/writersroom

### HELP WITH GRAMMAR

www.bbc.co.uk/skillswise/words/grammar/punctuation/commas/factsheet.shtml

### COMEDY WRITING

The Guardian writing website has comedy writing contributions from Richard Herring and Catherine Tate. www.guardian.co.uk/books/series/howtowrite

### STARTING A BLOG

wordpress.com

www.blogger.com

### THE COMEDY UNIT

www.comedyunit.co.uk

### OPEN ACCESS RADIO SHOW

*Newsjack* writers' guide. www.bbc.co.uk/programmes/b00kvs8r

### SCRIPT TEMPLATES

Script smart. www.bbc.co.uk/writersroom/scriptsmart

### POSTING A NOVEL ONLINE

Authonomy, run by HarperCollins, has a separate section for comedy. Post your work and get feedback from other writers. www.authonomy.com

### COPYRIGHT INFORMATION

www.patent.gov.uk

# Appendix A: full texts of examples

---

## Observational stand-up – Chapter 6

LADIES AND GENTLEMEN, WE APOLOGIZE FOR THE
DELAY...

*The cleaning lady enters, with mop and bucket.*

I know you're waiting for the bloke what juggles with vibrators, but
one of 'em's gone missing so, they've asked me to fill in. I don't why
because I'm only the cleaner, but it turns out the singer's got a sore
throat and the comedian won't come out of the loo. Men eh!

I've got nothing against men, mind, but I seen in the papers, them
scientists has worked out that men can only do one thing at a time
while women, right, women are what's called multifunctional.

Now what that means is a women can cook the breakfast, delouse
the dog, change the spark plug on the motor mower and do the kids'
homework all at the same time. But men can only do one thing. And
if he's scratching his head, well don't expect him to do nothing else.
Blimey we didn't need no scientist to tell us that did we? I think we'd
worked that one out hadn't we girls.

And I don't want to go on about sex, I leave that to the Women's
Institute, but you know what it's like don't you, you've got the man
shouting yes yes, while the women is getting on with her orgasm,
writing a shopping list, **and** trying to decide whether to go to Venice
or Venezuela for next year's holiday. Oh, and if it's Monday morning
she's probably changing the sheets and if it's Saturday she'll be
stripping the wall paper off with a chisel, ready to start decorating.

And talking of chisels – don't men ever go mad if you use one instead
of a screwdriver? I mean what's the big deal; they look the same
don't they? Anyway I was only scraping out the oven, no call for him
making all that fuss.

'Course he still thinks that sort of thing is woman's work along with
hoovering, gardening and servicing the car. So don't give me all that

New Man stuff. He says he done his bit when he wrote the cheque for the dishwasher. So why is it that as fast as I put the plates in he takes them out again and just ever so slightly rearranges them? What's that all about then?

Of course we are told it's all in the genes. I seen on the Internet that them scientists have mapped the Genome. I can see you're surprised I use the Internet. Well, I am one of them silver sufferers. You see it's us women what are into this hands-on technology. Men buy the computers, right, and they boast about the size of their rams and hard drives or whatever, but it's us women what work out how to use 'em. I tell you I roar down that information superhighway so fast it's a wonder I haven't been booked for speeding.

But back to the genes. Well I'm not no scientist but I could have identified one for them. It's that one what men share with animals. You know like when dogs meet up. No not that one, come on let's keep it clean.

No, it's the one with the urinals, right? Can you ever get a man to go past a urinal, no you can't. They've only got to see the magic word 'gents' and they're in there, leaving you standing outside looking like a lemon. I mean they don't really want to go. They can't want to go. They've been in every urinal since you've left home, there can't be nothing left. No, what they're doing, right, is they are marking territory, just like animals do. Each little splash on some broken filthy bit of porcelain says, 'this is mine, I was here'. And if they can't find a gents a large tree will do.

But I never say nothing. Live and let live, that's what I say. 'Course he doesn't see it that way. I says to him, I put up with your urinals, the least you can do is put up with my knickers. When we packs for a holiday we counts them out don't we girls? One for every day we're away, and a spare pair to carry in our handbags in case the luggage goes to Australia instead of Austria.

But what if we haven't got enough pairs? No problem, we'll wash some out while we're away won't we? So we just pop in our handbag a washing line, two dozen clothes pegs, a large packet of soap powder, fabric softener, a travelling iron and a bottle of distilled water. I tell you my handbag has often weighed more than my suitcase. Then we spend every morning hand washing everything we wore the day before just to be on the safe side. Well it's compulsive isn't it? The washing dries so well out there.

The old man's hammering on the bathroom door wanting to know when we're going down the beach. But we ignores him because we knows this is just a code for saying 'I want to mark territory in every foreign urinal I can', so we carries on buffing up the underwear with a nail brush. One holiday I come home with a suitcase full of clean clothes. I didn't see much of Marbella, but I can always look at his photographs. Mostly urinals of course.

His proud boast is that he is multilingual and he's right, he knows the word for gents in 17 languages although when he thinks we are going to visit Outer Mongolia is anybody's guess.

Still it's good for men to have a hobby isn't it and at least his doesn't cost any money. And why is that? Why do women have to pay and not men? It's one of those strange facts of life such as bread always falling butter-side down even when you're using Flora.

Hang on a minute, I can see the juggler's waving a vibrator over his head. So here's the act you've been waiting for...

---

## Character voice – Chapter 7

### *SAVING MONEY IN THESE STRAIGHTENED TIMES*

The credit crunch has hit all of us terribly hard, but I put on the old thinking cap and, as usual, I came up with a simply brilliant idea. It came to me in a flash – instead of popping across to Tuscany as per usual we would buy a 'motorized caravan' and save absolutely heaps of money. Bertie and I took our first trip over the Bank Holiday and had a perfectly splendid time. If you too are thinking of joining the merry band of motoring caravanners then here are a few little tips.

Firstly there is no need to go to all the trouble and expense of procuring hothouse lilies, (although by all means, if the gardener is able to provide them, you may as well enjoy their scent). But a few blooms from the rose garden in a simple cut glass vase will provide an elegant focal point for your living area. I designed a shelf to fit in the gap between the washroom wall and the TV cupboard.

Making the shelf was perfectly simple – there is a little man in the village who does all that sort of thing for one, and of course his wife is quite capable of making the new velvet curtains with swags and pelmets to replace the rather mean window dressings supplied with the camping van. While she had the Singer out it took very little extra effort for her to add the finishing touches to the four-poster that her husband had cleverly inserted into the space previously occupied by the very inadequate bed arrangement.

Do not, of course, pack the best china. The Sèvres dinner service is hardly appropriate and you can 'rough it' perfectly well with the second best Royal Worcester. One little tip that is well worth remembering is that grandma's silver teapot is unbreakable and ideal for a camping 'brew-up', as I believe it's called.

However many berths you have in your motoring caravan it is simply foolish to allow the butler to use one of them. The thing to do is to send the man on ahead with a pup tent, which will be quite adequate for his needs. With judicious planning it should be possible for him to serve one's breakfast at home and be on the camping site ready with luncheon just as one arrives.

And finally do not waste part of your precious payload carrying logs, kindling and firelighters. Try as you might you won't find a fireplace anywhere in a motor caravanette – something of an oversight that I intend to write to the manufacturers about. Poor Bertie had to stick his feet under the grill to achieve his favourite toasty warm sensation in his lower limbs.

I think you'll find that if you follow my advice you'll have a perfectly charming time in your van without spending a fortune, and still manage to live in the style to which we are all accustomed. However I don't recommend staying away from home for too long – after a week without fingerbowls even the strongest among us begins to quail.

---

## Sketch – Chapter 8

### FUNERAL FUN

A woman enters a funeral parlour.

*Undertaker:*   *May one be of assistance?*

*Woman:*   *Um... yes... it's a bit awkward.*

*Undertaker:*   *Modom has come to make arrangements for the dear departed? Rest assured, we are professionals.*

*Woman:*   *No, no, it's not that...*

**Undertaker:** *Modom is aware that this is a funeral parlour?*

**Woman:** (Angry) *Is it? Are you sure?* (Makes an effort at self-control. Produces a piece of paper.) *Actually it's about this bill of yours…*

**Undertaker:** (Taking the bill from her) *Ah yes. Funeral of Mr Johnson. I take it Modom is here on behalf of Mrs. Johnson?*

**Woman:** *Yes. She's my aunt.* (Beat) *It is a lot of money.*

**Undertaker:** *Mrs Johnson requested our top of the range funeral. The Jeeves.*

**Woman:** *Yes. You see, she is rather elderly. I'm not sure that she entirely understood the, er, the implications.*

**Undertaker:** *And then there is the extra charge for the services of the embalmer. Did you view the deceased in our Chapel of Jest?*

**Woman:** *Yes. Quite a shock.*

**Undertaker:** *So very lifelike. One almost expects the deceased to leap out of the coffin…*

**Woman:** *…and say 'Mr Grimsdale!'*

**Undertaker:** *Ah yes, you had the Norman Wisdom. Very impressive.*

**Woman:** *Considering my uncle was 6'3" and 16 stone.*

**Undertaker:** *A triumph of the embalmer's art. Only possible when expense is no object.*

**Woman:** *It certainly wasn't cheap. And did we really need two priests for the service?*

**Undertaker:** *That is standard with the Jeeves.* (Woman looks puzzled) *For the dead parrot sketch at the altar?* (Does a bad imitation of John Cleese) *'This is an ex-parrot'?*

**Woman:** (not amused) *Yes. I was there. I think we'd have preferred it without the, er, frills.*

**Undertaker:** *Is Modom referring to our basic funeral, the Coco? It lacks the richness of the Jeeves, but the priest does wear a red nose and a revolving bow tie instead of his dog collar. A little obvious perhaps but most effective for a certain class of person.*

**Woman:** *It's just that it's not what we were expecting.*

**Undertaker:** *No? Surely Mrs Johnson understood the nature of our service to the bereaved?* (He reveals a poster on the wall which reads 'we put the FUN back in FUNERAL')

**Woman:** *My aunt just wanted to do the best for her husband.*

**Undertaker:** *Quite so Modom. The Jeeves was clearly the most suitable. Everything of the best. Finest mahogany coffin, very solid...*

**Woman:** *...that's true. The poor chap had quite a struggle to saw it in half.* (She takes out her credit cards) *Look, I just want to pay the bill and forget about the whole thing. How much altogether?*

**Undertaker:** *That all depends on Modom's final decision. Regarding the ashes?* (He produces three identical urns from beneath the counter)

**Woman:** *Which one is it?*

**Undertaker:** *That one.* (He takes the lid off, shows her the ashes, replaces the lid) *Keep your eye on it.* (He swaps them round rapidly) *Choose one.*

**Woman:** *Er... that one?*

**Undertaker:** *Sure?*

**Woman:** *Yes. No. Oh, that one.* (She opens an urn. A boxing glove on a spring pops out)

**Undertaker:** *Modom wasn't paying attention was Modom? It's this one of course.* (He gives her the correct urn) *We can arrange disposal if required.*

**Woman:** (Clutching the urn protectively) *I don't want my uncle turned into sneezing powder!*

**Undertaker:** *Ah, very funny Modom. I'm afraid the ashes of deceased persons would never meet the required standard for sneezing powder. We merely place the ashes in the Garden of Remembrance.*

**Woman:** *No tricks? No jokes?*

**Undertaker:** *Indeed no. Unless you count...but it is a very small one.*

**Woman:** *A very small what?*

**Undertaker:** *A very small rollercoaster. Like the rest of the rides. Of course we do have rather a large Haunted House.*

| Woman: | More a Funfair of Remembrance really. I don't think my uncle would have wanted that. |
|---|---|
| Undertaker: | Was the deceased a little lacking in humour perhaps? |
| Woman: | You can say that again. He was a traffic warden. Very zealous. Even gave me a ticket once! |
| Undertaker: | Dear dear. |
| Woman: | I was picking my aunt up from the doctor's. His wife! She was on crutches at the time. And I was only giving her a lift because he was too mean to pay for a taxi. |

They both stare at the urn.

| Woman: | Bastard. |
|---|---|
| Undertaker: | Ex-bastard. |
| Woman: | He didn't like Norman Wisdom you know. Well he didn't like any of them. Couldn't take a joke. He would have hated that funeral. Hated it. (She smiles) |
| Undertaker: | Modom is feeling better? |
| Woman: | Oh yes. Yes indeed. |

She laughs. The undertaker looks smug.

*END*

---

## Sitcom – Chapters 9, 10 and 11

### THE HOUSE OF RELAXATION BY LESLEY BOWN AND ANN GAWTHORPE

*Note: for performance we changed Laura's name to Eve and called the piece Adam 'n' Eve.*

**MOVING DAY**

SCENE 1. INT DAY. THE RECEPTION AREA

**Stuart is sitting cross-legged meditating and reciting a mantra. Wendy enters carrying several box files. She drops the files on the desk, looks at Stuart, he doesn't react. She puts one CD in the computer and one CD in the sound system. Loud music blares out. Stuart leaps to his feet, turns off music.**

| STUART: | That's like, you know, really really dangerous? |
|---|---|
| WENDY: | If I was going to attack you Stuart, I'd use something sharper than the Spice Girls. |

Adam enters carrying cardboard box.

ADAM:   Hey, people, where'd the music go?

WENDY:   He doesn't like it.

ADAM:   That's cool. Tell ya what kid, run out and buy us some new sounds. Something really peppy and zippy.

STUART:   You mean, like, the music from Rainbow?

ADAM:   No, no, something, you know, young and zappy. Like us. Something nice and loud.

STUART:   I don't think Laura will like that. She likes everything peaceful. (Picks up CD from desk, reads label) 'Birdsong in the rainforest'. We usually have that in the mornings. (He puts the CD in the player)

FX:   twitterings

ADAM:   No no no no no. (To Wendy) Break out the Oasis kiddo. Let's get some atmos in here.

STUART:   No, that's no good, look, (picks up brochure from desk, reads) 'The House of Relaxation is a haven of quiet in the midst of city turmoil' Haven of quiet, right?

ADAM:   Well now it's gonna be an oasis of, er, Oasis.

STUART:   You can't do that. Supposing someone comes through the door right, and their aura is all, like ragged, and it needs smoothing out? You can't do that kind of thing with your head full of noise.

WENDY:   This is never going to work Adam. We can't share an office with a bunch of loonies, we just can't.

ADAM:   I need to be here. Keep an eye on things. Aunty Margaret would have wanted it.

Laura enters, tragic.

LAURA:   Did I hear someone say... Margaret? (Sobs)

STUART:   Now look what you've done. (To Laura) Let it all out, OK? (He passes her a box of tissues)

LAURA:   Yes, yes, I must, mustn't I?

ADAM:   Hey, we're all sad. She was my aunty, remember? I mean, you've only lost a business partner, I've lost family. Wendy, doughnuts, chop chop, there's a good girl.

WENDY: I keep telling you, I've a degree in computer science. I don't do cake shops.

LAURA: Still, it's not as if she's really gone.

ADAM: She's gone, believe me, I was at the funeral. So were you.

STUART: That's just like, her old body? It's not important.

ADAM: Not to you maybe sunshine, but she kind of needed it. Anyway the business was getting too much for her.

LAURA: No it wasn't.

ADAM: That's why she left it to me. Someone young...

WENDY: Huh!

ADAM: ...someone energetic. Someone with a vision for the new Millennium!

STUART: Laura sees visions, don't you Laura?

LAURA: Sometimes Stuart.

WENDY: I can see one right now. It's me down at the Job Centre.

LAURA: If only I knew why Margaret left her share to you Adam. It seems so odd.

STUART: Why don't you ask her?

LAURA: I will, the next time we talk I'll ask her.

WENDY: Adam, I'm telling you, this stuff really freaks me out.

STUART: That's because you're resisting. If you just kind of relax, and sort of let yourself go...

Stuart starts to massage Wendy's shoulders. She pushes him away.

ADAM: Wendy doesn't ever let anything go, do you Wendy?

LAURA: Ah, a deep-seated need for control.

WENDY: A deep-seated need for a bit of common sense, thank you very much. I mean, I thought working for Adam was like taking a daily trip up the yellow brick road...

ADAM: You know, I gave you a job when you were desperate...

LAURA: Desperate? She's got a degree in computer science.

ADAM: Total Mickey Mouse. Correspondence course. She knows all there is to know about BBC computers for schools, 1985 vintage. Don't you Wendy?

WENDY:     When I first knew you, you were in the software Stone Age.

LAURA:     I'm sensing a little bit of aggression here. Stuart, I think we need the grumpy hats.

Stuart takes bobble hats from a drawer, puts one on, starts handing out the others.

LAURA:     Now, why don't we all form a circle and...

WENDY:     Oh form your own circle. I've got work to do. (She exits)

ADAM:      Women, eh?

STUART:    How do you mean Adam?

LAURA:     Oh dear. I shall have to take five minutes out to calm myself. I'll be in my room Stuart. (She exits to her room)

ADAM:      That's what I mean. First sign of trouble and they're off. (He exits to Laura's room)

FX: phone rings. Stuart answers it.

STUART:    Hi, it's Stuart? How can I help? (Looks in appointment book) Sure, yeah, you can see a counsellor. Yeah she's really nice. No she never shouts. Really. Yeah you can come today. What about... two 'o' clock? Is that cool for you? Give us your name then. James? Oh, Mr Jamieson. Alright then. (Writes in the book)


SCENE 2. INT DAY. LAURA'S ROOM

ADAM:      Feeling better? Good, lovely. Now, about my office. This room will do me fine.

LAURA:     I don't know, that could be a little difficult. My work is confidential you see. (Adam picks up a crystal, fiddles with it)

ADAM:      I don't mean us to share it, I mean you to move into the other room.

LAURA:     But that's Margaret's room.

ADAM:      Was. (He puts the crystal in the wrong place)

LAURA:     She's your aunt. She wants you to have it. (She moves the crystal back)

ADAM: *But you were so much closer to her than me. I haven't even seen her since I was 15. She turned up on my birthday with some Winnie the Pooh slippers.*

LAURA: *I really do have to have this room.* (Closes her eyes, puts hand on chest) *This room speaks to me somehow. It's, it's... on my wavelength. It's got something...*

ADAM: *A fabulous view and plenty of space?* (He moves one of the easy chairs)

ADAM: *My desk could go here.*

LAURA: (opening eyes, glaring at Adam) *This is my room.* (She pushes the chair back into place) *Besides, it would mean moving Stuart to the other side of the reception area, and he'd never do that.*

ADAM: *I think you're missing something here Laura. You are his boss. That means, you tell him what to do, and then he does it.*

LAURA: *He's a Taurus. Very stubborn.*

ADAM: *I don't see why I should have that poky little room. We're equal partners.*

LAURA: *But Margaret liked that room.*

ADAM: *Well I don't.*

LAURA: *Oh, this is too much. First I lose Margaret, then my room.* (She sobs dramatically)

Adam and Laura glare at each other. Stuart enters

STUART: *Adam, somebody on the phone for you?*

Stuart exits. Adam looks exasperated, then exits. Laura rummages in her bag, desk, cupboard, etc. Pauses to think, lifts up statue of Buddha, finds key underneath.

## SCENE 3. INT DAY. RECEPTION AREA

Adam is on the phone. Wendy is unpacking. Stuart is at his desk. Laura enters from her room. She locks the door behind her.

STUART: *Oh no, locking the door, that's like, really bad karma? Like a prison or something?*

LAURA: *Try to think of it more as security. A safe place.*

ADAM: *Half-past nine then. Excellent.* (He hangs up)

ADAM:     Great. Now, Laura, about this little problem over rooms...

LAURA:    I don't see a problem Adam.

ADAM:     You only see solutions? That's my kind of thinking.

STUART:   No, she means defining something as a problem is a negative way of looking at it.

LAURA:    That's right. You could look on this a chance for personal growth Adam.

ADAM:     If I grew I wouldn't fit in the room, would I?

LAURA:    I'm sure you'll cope wonderfully. Now, anyone want anything from the Garden Centre?

WENDY:    You're going shopping? I thought your heart was broken?

LAURA:    I'll feel better if I go.

ADAM:     Shopping for grief therapy? Could be an interesting new marketing concept there.

STUART:   No, she's going to find Margaret.

ADAM:     At the Garden Centre?

WENDY:    Margaret is dead, you know that.

STUART:   Reincarnation. She told us she was sure she'd come back as a tree. We're going to plant her somewhere beautiful.

Laura exits.

ADAM:     Damn, I should have asked her to pick up the doughnuts. Wendy...

WENDY:    No.

ADAM:     This is crazy. Stuart, if Laura asked you to get doughnuts, you would, wouldn't you?

STUART:   No way.

WENDY:    See?

STUART:   White sugar is really really bad for you? I might get her carrot cake. She likes carrot cake.

ADAM:     OK, just this once, I will get the doughnuts. And if my new client turns up, Wendy, if it's not too much trouble, would you show him through to the office and get him a coffee?

WENDY:    No.

ADAM:   You've always done the coffee. You can't move the goalposts just like that.

WENDY:   It's not that. They haven't got any.

ADAM:   No coffee?

Stuart shakes his head.

WENDY:   Not allowed. Bad for us apparently.

ADAM:   Bad for you, coffee? Well I practically live off the stuff and I'm pretty normal, hey guys?

STUART:   I could rustle up a nice camomile tea. Very soothing.

ADAM:   Never mind. Just look after him. He's coming to consult the Millennium Maestro.

STUART:   Wow, is that a new therapy?

ADAM:   No, it's marketing. This is a brand new Millennium Stuart. Every business in the land needs a Millennium angle. And I'm the guy to do it. I help them maximize their Millennium marketing potential.

Stuart looks puzzled.

WENDY:   He means T-shirts. He puts the company name on T-shirts and calls that a Millennium angle. That's all.

ADAM:   That is not all, not by a very long shot.

WENDY:   OK, so he does biros as well.

ADAM:   Well now we're doing shopping trolleys, or will be if we land the account. The publicity potential of the shopping trolley has barely been scratched.

STUART:   I'll put him in the book then. (Opens appointment book) See, I've done a special column for your appointments, with a lilac line, because you're a lilac kind of person, OK Adam?

ADAM:   No it is not OK. For a start I'm red. Definitely red. Very red. (Rummages in box, produces electronic organizer) And all my appointments are in here. Wendy, I'll be busy all morning with this guy. (Passes her the organizer)

WENDY:   This is the 21st century Stuart. (She presses buttons)

VOICE:   You have no free time this morning. Have a nice day.

STUART:   Wow.

Adam takes organizer, puts it on desk next to appointment book. He exits.

WENDY:   *Where's the kettle?*

STUART:   (pointing) *In the kitchen. And the camomile tea is on the shelf.*

WENDY:   *I won't be needing that thank you very much.*

She exits to kitchen. Stuart looks at organizer, his hand hovers towards it.

FX:   phone rings. Stuart answers it.

STUART:   *Hi it's Stuart? (Beat) This morning? Er, are you sure you need to come twice in one day? That is Mr Jamieson, isn't it? (Looks in book) I've already got you in for two 'o' clock. No don't worry, it's easily done. Like I'm always turning up for work on a Sunday? Yeah, right. 'Bye.*

Stuart hangs up, turns back to organizer. Wendy enters with cup of hot water, he snatches his hand back.

STUART:   *Find it all right then?*

WENDY:   *It was a challenge, but I managed.* (She takes a jar of coffee from her bag, opens it, sniffs the aroma)

STUART:   *That's coffee!*

WENDY:   *So it is.* (She spoons some into her cup, stirs and inhales)

WENDY:   *Mmm, lovely. Bet you want some, don't you Stuart.*

STUART:   *No. And you told Adam, you said there wasn't any coffee.*

WENDY:   *No I didn't. I said I wouldn't make coffee for his client, and I said coffee wasn't allowed in here.*

STUART:   *You know what I mean.*

WENDY:   *This is my own personal coffee, which I paid for myself. If Adam wants coffee, he can get his own.* (She raises the cup to her lips, sips)

Adam enters with doughnuts, Wendy splutters and hides cup beneath her desk.

ADAM:   *I can smell coffee!*

STUART:   *She's got coffee. Under her desk.*

WENDY:   *Tell tale!*

ADAM: *Ah, I knew she'd look after me. Coffee Wendy please, I'll be in my office – and don't forget my client.* (He takes a doughnut, drops the bag on Wendy's desk, exits to his room.) *Wendy picks up coffee jar and exits to the kitchen. Stuart touches the organizer.*

VOICE: *You have no free time this morning. Have a nice day.*

Wendy looks out of kitchen.

WENDY: *Leave that alone! You haven't been trained to use it.*

STUART: *Sorry.*

WENDY: *Don't you touch it again.* (She disappears to kitchen briefly, enters with cup of coffee crosses to Adam's room, knocks, opens door)

FX: phone on Wendy's desk rings.

Before Stuart can answer it, Wendy exits from Adam's room and answers the phone.

WENDY: *Millennium Maestro. Ah good morning. Yes. Yes. Of course, no problem.* (She hangs up, presses buttons on organizer, crosses to Adam's office, knocks and enters)

SCENE 4. INT DAY. ADAM'S OFFICE

WENDY: *I just had your new client on the phone Adam. He's rearranged for this afternoon, about one-thirty.*

ADAM: *Okey-dokey.* (Leans back in chair) *Maybe I'll just catch some zeds.*

WENDY: *We've still got a lot of stuff at the old office Adam.*

ADAM: *Yeah.* (Takes car keys from pocket) *Tell you what, how'd you like to do it?*

WENDY: *No thanks.*

ADAM: (Holds out keys) *You'll get to drive the Beamer.*

WENDY: *I don't do removals.*

ADAM: *Why aren't I surprised. OK, I'll drive, but will you come and help? If it's not too much trouble of course.*

WENDY: *I don't know.*

ADAM: *Lunch is on me?*

WENDY: *Oh, alright.*

## SCENE 5. INT DAY. RECEPTION AREA

Adam and Wendy enter from Adam's office.

ADAM: *Hey, Stuart, kiddo, howja like to be in charge for a bit?*

STUART: *Oh no. Power corrupts you know.*

Wendy picks up piece of paper and pencil.

WENDY: *Just answer the phone and write down our messages. And don't touch that.* (Points to the organizer)

Adam and Wendy exit. Stuart hovers over organizer.

STUART: *It's like, covered in little buttons?* (He reaches out, and snatches his hand back) *I bet it takes loads of training. Months and months.* (He touches the organizer) *It can't be that hard.* (He presses a button)

VOICE: *You have no free time this morning.*

STUART: *Wow. It's just so easy.* (He touches another button)

VOICE: *Mr Jamieson is due at thirteen thirty hours.*

STUART: *Oh, wow, how did you know that? But you got the time wrong, you know?* (He presses buttons) *I just spoke to him on the phone right? He's coming at two.*

VOICE: *It is three twenty nine pm.*

STUART: *No it isn't.* (He presses another button)

VOICE: *It is your wife's birthday tomorrow. You are due for a dental check up. Mind the doors please.*

Stuart frantically presses buttons, nothing happens. Laura enters, carrying odd looking pot plant. Puts it on desk with great reverence.

LAURA: (brokenly) *Oh, Margaret!*

STUART: *Oh crumbs.*

## SCENE 6. INT DAY. RECEPTION AREA. CLOCK SHOWS 1.30

Laura is fussing over the plant. Wendy enters carrying box of files.

WENDY: *Ugh, what's that?*

LAURA: *It's Margaret.*

WENDY: *You said she was coming back as a tree.*

LAURA: *It's what she wants. I felt it as soon as I got into the Garden Centre. I was heading for the trees but I felt myself being sort of pulled, pulled...*

WENDY: *You probably got one of those trolleys with wonky wheels.*

LAURA: *She wants to be near us.* (To plant) *You do, don't you? She doesn't want to be planted out in some cold lonely field. This way is nicer.*

WENDY: *And cheaper. Well, keep it away from me, I'm allergic to the nasty things.* (She sneezes)

LAURA: *You should try to bond with her. Female solidarity is so important, don't you think dear?*

WENDY: *I am not bonding with a pot plant, however female it is.*

LAURA: *I used to look up to Margaret you know. She was a mother figure to me, with so much wisdom. I feel that I could do the same for you somehow.*

WENDY: *I've already got a mother, thank you very much.*

LAURA: *I could give you so much advice. Men for instance. I sense that your manner puts them off. Men like a women to be soft. Feminine.*

WENDY: *Now you do sound like my mother.*

LAURA: *And of course, however desperate you are, you must never let it show.*

WENDY: *I'm not desperate, I've got loads of boyfriends, actually, loads.*

LAURA: *There's nothing wrong with being a single woman Wendy. Look at me, I'm perfectly happy and fulfilled. I can be a role model for you.*

WENDY: *But you're heaps older than me!*

LAURA: *Not that much dear. Although I do have an instinct for handling men. Take Adam for instance. He's inclined to be a little bit dominant, don't you find?*

WENDY: *I'm not even 30 yet. Not for ages.*

LAURA: *That's why we can't let him have my room, do you see?*

Stuart enters with plant sprayer.

STUART:   *Look what I've bought for Margaret!*

LAURA:   *Just remember what I said. We must stick together, mustn't we?*

STUART:   *Where shall we put her?*

WENDY:   *Get rid of it, for goodness sake.*

LAURA:   *But this is where she needs to be. Margaret needs to be among us.*

STUART:   *Oh yes, she'll have to be here with us.*

WENDY:   *Well if she comes over here she'll get pruned.*

Laura and Stuart look at each other.

STUART:   *Look at that aura.*

LAURA:   *Mmm, I know. Grumpy hat I think Stuart.*

Stuart pulls out bobble hats.

WENDY:   *Whatever game this is, I'm not playing.*

LAURA:   *So much negative energy. I'm sure we can help you.*

WENDY:   *Please don't.*

STUART:   *But we always do this. Look,* (pulls on a hat) *see, when I'm wearing the hat, I'm taking time out from my anger.*

LAURA:   *Margaret and I always worked through our issues wearing our hats. When you take the hat off, you leave your issues behind you, in the hat.* (She puts on a hat)

**Wendy** throws her hat in waste paper basket.

WENDY:   *What you two weirdoes get up to is your business* (picks up papers) *if you'll excuse me, I've got photocopying to do.* (She exits)

LAURA:   *Poor girl.*

Laura removes hat and exits to her room. Stuart keeps his hat on. Stuart goes to the organizer and starts punching buttons.

STUART:   *Hi this is Stuart? Um, are you still feeling a bit confused?*

VOICE:   *You weigh 11 stone. You have aggressive tendencies.*

STUART:   *That's just so wrong.* (Shakes the organizer)

VOICE:   *Instruction accepted. All data has been removed.*

STUART:   *Oh no, oh no, I've broken it!* (Puts his hand to his chest, pants) *I'm having a panic attack! Paper bag! Paper bag!* (He sees the bag of doughnuts, picks it up, takes out one doughnut, looks round) *Plate! Plate!* (He exits to the kitchen)

A man, harassed, enters, talking on mobile phone.

MAN:   *...now listen to me laddie, it's time you bucked up your ideas.* (Beat) *Don't give me that. I'm just about to see this marketing consultant and I'll be back at the works in 45 minutes. I expect to find you there bright eyed and bushy tailed and wearing your overalls,* (beat) *I don't care if you have got an appointment with a counsellor. It's all nonsense. You cancel it and get on with some hard work, you hear me?* (Hangs up phone)

Stuart enters from the kitchen carrying doughnuts on a plate. He has sugar and jam all over his face.

MAN:   *I don't know what you lads are coming to.*

STUART:   *I'm sorry?*

MAN:   *Confused, he says. Needs to sort his head out he says.*

STUART:   *Aah.*

MAN:   *Now don't you take his side.*

STUART:   *OK.*

Silence. Man glares at Stuart.

MAN:   *I don't want to be a nuisance or possibly even force you to do your job but I do have an appointment. If it's not too much trouble.*

Stuart looks at organizer.

STUART:   *Who with?*

MAN:   *Well, whoever it is in this organization that sorts out problems.*

Stuart looks in the book.

STUART:   Er... Mr Jamieson?

MAN:   That's me.

STUART:   Come this way please. (He knocks on Laura's door and opens it)

STUART:   Mr Jamieson is here Laura.

MAN:   Wash your face laddie, it's covered in your lunch.

Man exits to Laura's room. Adam enters carrying box of files. Stuart is wiping his face with a tissue.

ADAM:   Everything OK Stuart?

STUART:   Er, well...

ADAM:   That's the way. (sees plant) What's that monstrosity?

STUART:   That's your aunty, Adam.

ADAM:   She never was much of a looker. Where's Wendy?

STUART:   Gone down to the photocopier.

ADAM:   That's a good sign. It means she's settling in. Stuart?

STUART:   Yes Adam?

ADAM:   Look, since it's just us guys together, can I speak frankly?

STUART:   OK.

ADAM:   Well I think Wendy would settle even better if she had her desk over there.

STUART:   It would be very crowded with two of us. And that side would be empty.

ADAM:   True. Well, maybe we could move your desk to where hers is now?

STUART:   But this is my side, I meditate on this side. No, it wouldn't work. Sorry.

ADAM:   It's just that I don't like to see Wendy upset. I have a bit of a soft spot where girls are concerned Stuart. You know how it is. I can't bear the tears.

STUART:   She makes you cry does she?

ADAM: No, Wendy's tears. You don't think I cry, do you?

STUART: Crying is healthy for us all Adam. Actually Wendy strikes me as someone who doesn't cry enough. She keeps it all bottled up inside. That's not good.

ADAM: OK. Well you can be the one to tell her. Let's see how you like that. Now if my client turns up Stuart, I don't suppose you'd make him a cup of… no never mind. Just show him through, would you? (He exits to his room)

SCENE 7. INT DAY. LAURA'S ROOM

Laura and the man are facing each other across a low table.

MAN: I didn't expect to be seeing a lass.

LAURA: Does that bother you?

MAN: Not if you know your stuff. Well, fire away.

LAURA: Hmmm. Is there anything you want to tell me?

MAN: How do you mean?

LAURA: I mean whatever you want me to mean.

MAN: Oh, ha, very clever, get me to do all the work, eh, I tell you what I want?

LAURA: Only if you want to.

MAN: Well, OK, I'll play your little game. I want a plan, that's what I want, I want it simple, I want it straightforward and I don't want it to cost too much.

LAURA: I see.

MAN: The question is, can you deliver? I'm not looking for some airy fairy arty farty nonsense. As far as I'm concerned a trolley is a trolley.

LAURA: I see. You see a trolley as a metaphor for life?

MAN: If it steers straight I'm a happy man.

LAURA: And does it? Does your trolley steer straight?

SCENE 8. INT DAY. THE RECEPTION AREA

Stuart is at the desk. Wendy enters carrying pile of photocopying.

WENDY: Stuart, would you say I looked desperate?

STUART: Oh no, you look very nice. Why?

WENDY: *Never mind.*

STUART: *By the way Wendy, I have something to tell you.* (He has the box of tissues ready)

WENDY: *What?*

STUART: *I'm afraid it won't be possible for you to move your desk over here.* (He pushes the tissues towards her)

WENDY: *OK.*

STUART: *I have to have my desk over here. I need to meditate, and I need to sit here, where the vibes are right, do you see?*

WENDY: *No.*

STUART: *Well I do just have to sit here. How do you feel about that?*

WENDY: *Fine.*

STUART: *Adam thought you might cry.*

WENDY: *Oh no. I never cry. I just get revenge.*

A scruffy young man enters.

WENDY: *Can I help you?*

YOUNG MAN: *I've got an appointment. I think.*

WENDY: *You don't think I look desperate, do you?*

YOUNG MAN: *Oh, have we started?*

WENDY: *Forget it.* (She presses organizer)

VOICE: *You have no appointments.*

WENDY: *That can't be right.*

Stuart looks in the book.

STUART: *I've got a Mrs Hudson, but that's tomorrow.*

WENDY: (pressing buttons) *Somebody's been messing around with this.*

YOUNG MAN: *I'm not Mrs Hudson. I think.*

STUART: *It was me. Sorry.*

YOUNG MAN: *You're Mrs Hudson.?*

STUART: *No, I'm Stuart.*

YOUNG MAN: *Perhaps I thought I was Mrs Hudson when I made the call. I do get confused.*

WENDY: *Why can't you just leave things alone?*

YOUNG MAN: *Sorry.*

WENDY: *Not you. Him*

YOUNG MAN: *Sorry.*

STUART: *I'm really really sorry Wendy. I'll do anything to make it up to you.*

WENDY: *Fine. There's still plenty of stuff in the boot of Adam's car. Off you go.*

Young man starts to exit. Wendy holds up her hand to stop him. Stuart exits. Adam enters from his room.

ADAM: *Ah, good afternoon, Mr Jamieson?*

YOUNG MAN: *Er…possibly.*

Adam shakes him vigorously by the hand.

ADAM: *Let me say at once you've come to the right place. We can solve all your problems.*

YOUNG MAN: *Oh good.*

ADAM: *You sounded older on the phone. One of our younger entrepreneurs, eh?*

YOUNG MAN: *Probably.*

ADAM: *Shall I take your, er, anorak?* (He takes it and hangs it up) *Well if you'd like to go in. Make yourself comfortable.*

Young man exits to Adam's room. Adam crosses to Wendy.

ADAM: *I want you to get your desk over that side.*

WENDY: *I know.*

ADAM: *Use your feminine wiles on Stuart. He'll be a pushover.*

WENDY: *Perhaps you'd like me to sleep with him? Apparently I'm desperate.*

ADAM: *No need to go over the top. A few tears should do the trick.*

## SCENE 9. INT DAY. LAURA'S ROOM

The businessman is leaning back in his chair, tie undone.

LAURA: *So what would you say was the real problem here?*

MAN: *It all started with the Millennium.*

LAURA:   Mmm. A lot of people were worried about that.

MAN:   Well of course. For a start there was the bug.

LAURA:   You're worried about a bug?

MAN:   I handed the whole thing over to the boy. You see, I wanted him to take some responsibility for once. It didn't work. Gormless, that's what he is. My own son.

LAURA:   I see.

MAN:   I said to him, I said, it's the Millennium. You'll have to shape up laddie. Ask yourself, what does it mean? Where are we going?

LAURA:   Those are big questions.

MAN:   Aye, but they have to be answered. I said to the boy, we're standing still, we can't afford to stand still. There's no standing still in the world of trolleys.

LAURA:   Because of the wheels?

SCENE 10. INT DAY. ADAM'S ROOM

The young man is sitting on the couch, surrounded by cardboard boxes.

ADAM:   ... and if you follow me so far it's a simple question of setting up a cost benefit analysis and transferring the results into a reality-based action plan.

YOUNG MAN:   Do you mind if I lie down?

ADAM:   Well, no, you go ahead.

The young man stretches out on the couch among the boxes.

YOUNG MAN:   I'm afraid I'm not very good at action. A bit indecisive.

ADAM:   And that's why you need me. I can make it all perfectly simple and smooth for you.

YOUNG MAN:   Oh good.

ADAM:   We ought to start by identifying the problem and breaking it down into a series of core components.

YOUNG MAN:   It all started with the Millennium.

ADAM:   I know.

YOUNG MAN: *I knew you would. You make me feel, somehow...*
*safe.*

ADAM: *It's a simple question of prioritizing.*

YOUNG MAN: *I don't know. It was all so uncertain. People*
*couldn't even agree on the date you know. We*
*could still be heading for Armageddon.*

ADAM: *Out of town shopping centre? Perfect.*

YOUNG MAN: *It could be the end of the world as we know it.*

ADAM: *Oh yes. It's the start of a wonderful new world.*

YOUNG MAN: *Is it?*


## SCENE 11. INT DAY. LAURA'S ROOM

The man is lying on the couch, shoes off, Laura is giving him
reflexology.

MAN: *Oh, ah, mmm.*

LAURA: *That's better, isn't it?*

MAN: *That's wonderful. Just wonderful.*

LAURA: *No more worrying about the Millennium?*

MAN: *Oh no.*

LAURA: *No more worrying about your son?*

MAN: *Oh no. He's a good boy. Sorry, I mean young man.*

LAURA: *That's right.*

MAN: *It's not his fault he doesn't like the trolleys.*

LAURA: *No indeed.*


## SCENE 12. INT DAY. ADAM'S ROOM

Adam is squashed in the corner, standing by a flip chart with
complicated diagrams. The young man is watching from the couch,
from behind a wall of boxes.

ADAM: *So, if we follow the demand curve to here, taking account*
*of the profitability axis, what do we get?*

YOUNG MAN: (panicky) *I don't know, I don't know.*

ADAM: *T-shirts, right? We get T-shirts.*

YOUNG MAN:   *T-shirts? Not biros?*

ADAM:   *You're beginning to get the hang of this.*


## SCENE 13. INT DAY. RECEPTION AREA

Wendy and Stuart are at their desks.

WENDY:   *So, tell me, Stuart, what do you do in your spare time?*

STUART:   *Oh, you know. The usual.*

WENDY:   *The usual what?*

STUART:   *Oh, you know. Yoga. Tai Chi. And Laura wants me to go to assertiveness.*

WENDY:   *Just a normal regular guy then?*

STUART:   *Yes.*

WENDY:   *And do you really believe all this stuff?*

STUART:   *All what stuff?*

WENDY:   *Oh, auras and karma and coming back as a tatty pot plant.*

STUART:   *Of course I do. In fact reading auras is, like, my speciality.*

WENDY:   *So, what happened to Margaret's aura? Does it stay with her? Has her plant got it?*

STUART:   *I don't know. She doesn't seem to be on my wavelength.*

WENDY:   *Oh dear.*

STUART:   *Laura can always make contact.*

WENDY:   *The thing is Stuart, er, how does it come through? Do you hear voices in your head?*

STUART:   *Oh no, nothing like that. Laura says she just gets a sort of feeling, and somehow she knows what the person wants.*

WENDY:   *That might explain it...*

STUART:   *What? Can you hear Margaret? Can you?*

WENDY:   *Well, I'm not sure. I just get this feeling* (picks up plant) *that I have to move it, er, her, over to this side* (walks across) *oh no* (stops near her desk) *now I'm getting a feeling... that she doesn't want to upset anyone. What can it mean?*

STUART: (excited) *She wants to be on your desk, it must be that.*

WENDY: *But then what about that other feeling? Just when I got next to my desk... I can't explain it. Help me Stuart.*

STUART: (bitterly) *I don't know. Why should she talk to you? She never even met you. It's not fair.*

WENDY: (fakes a sneeze) *I know, it's my allergy. She doesn't want to set it off. Was she a very caring person Stuart?*

STUART: *I suppose.*

WENDY: *Look, let's try something. Come and stand here* (she leads him to her desk, puts the plant in his hand) *oh yes, that's better. She likes that. But it's still not quite right. Here, try this.* (She gives Stuart the appointment book, and moves across to Stuart's desk. They have now changed places) *That's it! Oh Stuart, she loves being over there with you.*

SCENE 14. INT DAY. ADAM'S ROOM

The young man is standing up, excited. Adam is sitting on the couch.

YOUNG MAN: *So what you're saying is, the aim of the game is to make money?*

ADAM: *Now we're cooking with gas!*

YOUNG MAN: *And when you've made it, you can spend it?*

ADAM: *Whatever you want. Fast car, penthouse flat. New anorak.*

YOUNG MAN: *My dad says it's all about getting up early and shouting at people.*

ADAM: *Nah, that's the old way. I'm showing you the bright new shiny Millennium way. Together we can make a fortune.*

YOUNG MAN: *Oh I won't be needing you* (holds out hand) *I'll be off then. Cheerio.* (He exits)

ADAM: *Hang on, wait...* (He exits)

SCENE 15. INT DAY. RECEPTION AREA

Wendy is working at Stuart's desk. Stuart has the plant on Wendy's desk. The young man is putting on his anorak. Adam enters.

ADAM: *Right, when shall we meet again?*

YOUNG MAN: *Look, I just told you. I can do this on my own.*

ADAM:   But I've got the marketing expertise...

YOUNG MAN:   It seems perfectly simple to me. I'm not paying you to run up a few T-shirts. I'm going to need all my money, aren't I, eh? There's the anorak for a start, that won't come cheap.

ADAM:   Shall I pencil you in for Wednesday? Wendy, check if I've got a window on Wednesday would you?

The man enters from Laura's room, followed by Laura. He is holding a flower.

MAN:   Can I come again? Next week?

LAURA:   Of course you can. Whenever you want.

YOUNG MAN:   Dad! What are you doing here?

MAN:   My boy! (He embraces the young man tearfully)

YOUNG MAN:   (pushing him away) That's enough of that.

MAN:   No you don't understand. When I came here I thought I was going to see a marketing consultant...

ADAM:   He's my client!

MAN:   ...but now I see that none of that matters.

ADAM:   (to Laura) You stole my client!

LAURA:   I did not. He found me.

MAN:   I've been too hard on you son. Can you forgive me?

ADAM:   (to man) Look, why don't you come into my office, and we can get to grips with this thing.

YOUNG MAN:   (to man) I haven't got time for this right now dad. But we must meet up soon. Why don't we do lunch? Give me a call, OK? Ciao. (He exits)

ADAM:   (to man) I'm afraid there's been a bit of a mix-up. I can't think how.

MAN:   Never mind, it doesn't matter. (He gives Adam the flower) (To Laura) I'll see you next week my dear.

ADAM:   No!

Man exits

LAURA:   Things always turn out for the best Adam, if you let them.

ADAM: *No they don't. Somewhere along the line I've lost the chance to make a pot of money.*

LAURA: *Oh, Adam, money isn't important. Possessions aren't important. You'll come to see that one day.* (She turns towards her room)

ADAM: *Hang on, hang on. I think I'll be having that room after all.*

LAURA: *What makes you think that?*

ADAM: *Look. Wendy and Stuart have swapped. So now it makes sense for us to swap. It's only a room Laura. Possessions aren't important.*

LAURA: *Stuart, what on earth were you thinking of?*

STUART: *It wasn't me. It was Margaret.*

LAURA: *What?*

ADAM: *Oh aunty, thank you.*

WENDY: *Yes I'm sorry Laura, Margaret told me she wanted to be on this side. And of course, with my allergy, well, you know, I'm desperate not to set it off.*

LAURA: *Allergy? Hah!*

WENDY: *I'm sensing a bit of aggression here. Hat Stuart, quick.*

STUART: (claps his hands) *Cool.*

Stuart pulls out bobble hats, gives one to Laura who tosses it aside, and one to Wendy.

ADAM: (to Laura) *So, I'll start moving my stuff. Key please.*

Stuart gives him a hat, he looks puzzled, but puts it on.

LAURA: (to Wendy) *I thought we bonded. Women should be able to resolve their issues Wendy.*

STUART: *Put yours on Wendy.*

WENDY: *Oh no, not me.* (She puts the hat over the plant) *Resolve it with her.*

Laura seizes the plant and hat and dumps them in the wastepaper bin.

*END*

# Index

# Image credits